JERRY COKER is Associate Professor of Music at the University of Tennessee. He is also the author of several other books on jazz, including *The Jazz Idiom* and *Improvising Jazz*, and he has toured as featured tenor saxophonist with the Woody Herman orchestra.

LISTENING
TO
JAZZ

JERRY COKER

A SPECTRUM BOOK

PRENTICE-HALL, INC., Englewood Cliffs, N.J. 07632

Library of Congress Cataloging in Publication Data

Coker, Jerry.
  Listening to jazz.

  (A Spectrum Book)
  Includes discographies.
  1. Jazz music—Instruction and study.   I. Title.
MT86.C59   785.4′2   77-17309
ISBN 0-13-537217-8
ISBN 0-13-537209-7 pbk.

A Spectrum Book

10 9 8 7 6 5 4 3

Printed in the United States of America

Prentice-Hall International, Inc., *London*
Prentice-Hall of Australia Pty. Limited, *Sydney*
Prentice-Hall of Canada, Ltd., *Toronto*
Prentice-Hall of India Private Limited, *New Delhi*
Prentice-Hall of Japan, Inc., *Tokyo*
Prentice-Hall of Southeast Asia Pte. Ltd., *Singapore*
Whitehall Books Limited, *Wellington, New Zealand*

CONTENTS

PREFACE

This book was written in the belief that jazz music, when approached with understanding and an absence of prejudice, appeals to virtually anyone and everyone. Reaching an understanding of the music, though, can be difficult for the average listener. A number of fine books written to aid the growing jazz musician are often too technical in language and approach to serve the reader who simply wants to know what is transpiring in the average jazz performance. Other books that are directed to the jazz listener fail to give the reader understanding of the music. A chronological approach to jazz history doesn't quite work. The reader ends up with a "who's who" knowledge of jazz, laced with a lot of unnecessary facts and a gross absence of information that would enable the reader to perceive jazz performances in the same manner as the performers themselves.

This, then, is not a book about the great bands of Count Basie and Duke Ellington, nor about the commercial successes of the Benny Goodman or Stan Kenton bands or the

Dave Brubeck Quartet. Nor is it a book about great singers, such as Billie Holiday, Ella Fitzgerald, and Sarah Vaughn, although all those performers have contributed considerably to the field. The real crux of the matter lies in achieving an understanding of improvisation, the creative source for *all* jazz. The main thrust of this book is, then, to help the reader understand the objectives and accomplishments of the best of the jazz improvisers with a bare minimum of technical language.

As the *Smithsonian Collection of Jazz,* edited and annotated by Martin Williams is, in my estimation, by far the best collection of jazz recordings ever assembled, I have referred the reader to selections from that collection whenever possible. The *Smithsonian Collection* is reasonably priced at $24.50, which includes six records and an excellent guide to using the collection, written by Martin Williams, along with many explanatory notes about the music. The package may be ordered from Smithsonian Institution, P.O. Box 1641, Washington, D.C., 20013.

Appendices are provided in this book to help the reader retain a clear focus on names, dates, and terms. Appendix A is a chronology of players, Appendix B is a condensed overview of jazz history, and Appendix C is a glossary of terms used in the book.

It is my sincerest hope that every reader will come to understand and feel the universal appeal of jazz music and that this book will bring the listener closer, in spirit, to the attitudes, conceptions, and expressions of the extraordinary musicians discussed in these pages.

FOREWORD BY JAMEY AEBERSOLD

Jerry Coker has been a leader in jazz education since he wrote *Improvising Jazz* in 1964. Since that time many people have written on the subject, but not all have the authority that he possesses. Jerry is a talented performer, composer, teacher, and lecturer, and his books are a projection of his beautiful personality.

Listening to Jazz fills a need for all those students and teachers who long for a text which will guide the listener as well as the performer to a closer understanding of what it means to improvise with music in today's jazz idiom. I find this book to be most helpful in that it allows the reader access to thoughts previously unrecorded in print. Jazz styles have often been difficult to verbalize, but I have found this book to be extremely concise and direct.

Contrary to public opinion of years past, you *can* become more knowledgable by reading, talking, and discussing jazz music in order to gain insight into the performers' improvised solos. *Listening to Jazz* will open new doors for you, the reader. And if you are a performing musician, I know this book will touch your playing and make things possible that may have been previously unthinkable.

FOREWORD
BY
DAVID BAKER

Once again Jerry Coker has discovered a void in the area of jazz educational materials and has expertly filled that void. This new book is so necessary and obvious in its import that one must wonder why someone hasn't written it before. Of course, there are very few musicians with the qualifications to conceptualize and bring to fruition a book of this magnitude. Jerry Coker is one of them.

Aside from the book's obvious value to jazz performers (amateurs and professionals), critics, historians and jazz dilletantes, it should be mandatory reading for *every* music teacher.

In addition to providing an excellent method for listening to and evaluating jazz performances in any style and from any era, the book also makes available excellent lists of quintessential performances on record, music portraits of six major figures, a list of basic tune types, and an excellent glossary.

The sections dealing with music habits, clichés, originality, repairing errors, and so on are particularly outstanding.

This book is a welcome addition to jazz literature and is absolutely essential to all who are seriously interested in contemporary music.

1

LISTENING
TO
JAZZ

Music is an art form that combines pitches with rhythms.[1] Although it can be prepared on paper in a notated fashion, a musical composition does not become music until the moment of performance, when it becomes *sound*. Music is an *aural* art. After the performance, when the sounds have ceased, the music ends, even though the written score, the instruments of performance, and the performers still exist. Only in the *memory* does the music continue to exist in the minds of musicians and their audience.

The aural memory, however, is not to be dismissed lightly. In fact, it may be the most powerful agent contributing to the success of the phenomenon we call music. It is the memory which enables us to hear music *inwardly*, replaying endlessly the sound sensations heard in prior listening experiences. Only a repeat of the aural experience itself can improve upon the impression made by the version that is

---

[1] Vibrational frequencies of sound, or simply what we call "notes" in music.

1

replayed in the memory. Hence it is largely the memory that enables us, by transforming repetition into familiarity, to develop a longing to repeat and enlarge the aural experience through recordings and live performance).

Dr. Joseph Murphy states that "Man is what he thinks all day."[2] Concurrently, religious and philosophical disciplines and goals are often achieved through repetitive affirmations. And so it is in music: We are what we hear all day, including live or recorded performances as well as what we hear inwardly through memory. There will be significant differences among individuals exposed to the same diet of listening, in that their attitudes, understanding, and personal involvement with music will vary. Their memory replays will vary with respect to selectivity, according to personal tastes and reactions. Our musical personalities can best be understood in terms of what we have heard in performance and what our memory chooses to replay inwardly.[3]

There are many musical *styles* to hear, each having given rise to great performances and each possessing stylistic validity. Stylistic snobbery in music is entirely unnecessary. It may, in some cases, be necessary for a musician to focus on a particular style for a lifetime, in order to achieve mastery or success in that style. But he must not, in the process, become negative toward other styles. A great performer in any style will have certain standards in common with others of his kind:

1. *Craftsmanship*
   a. understanding of musical fundamentals
   b. instrumental/vocal techniques
   c. well-developed ear
2. *Awareness* (from listening to others in field)

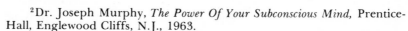

[2]Dr. Joseph Murphy, *The Power Of Your Subconscious Mind,* Prentice-Hall, Englewood Cliffs, N.J., 1963.

[3]For a more complete discussion of the potential of the ear for development, see pp. 17-22 of *The Jazz Idiom,* Coker, Prentice-Hall, Englewood Cliffs, 1975.

3. *Creativity*
4. *Spirit* (emotional drive, appropriateness)

Frequently the listener is confronted with a reputedly great performance he cannot understand or evaluate, usually because his memory bank of aural experiences does not encompass what he is now hearing. Perhaps the style is unfamiliar or the techniques too complex or too different from what he's heard previously. Chances are that if the listener had gathered, stored, and replayed the aural experiences that were in the minds of the performers, awareness and familiarity would have urged him onto a path of patient acceptance, understanding, and perhaps even approval and enjoyment. The gulf sometimes created between the performer and his audience is often directly related to the differences in their listening habits and choices. A performer tires of being held back, and his audience tires of feeling ignorant. The solution lies in the performer's desire to communicate and the audience's desire to understand.

WHAT IS JAZZ?

Up to now we have been discussing music in general, the importance of listening, memory replay, and standards of performance, as these points relate to *all* styles of music. But as this book is about jazz music in particular, a definition is now in order:

Jazz. A musical style that evolved in the United States around 1900, chiefly played by Afro-Americans, though the music has since been produced and consumed interracially and internationally. Jazz was, in the earliest stages, a brewing of many stylistic influences—African rhythms and "blue tones," European instruments and harmonies, marches, dance music, church music, and ragtime—all played with an exaggerated, emotional pulse (or beat). The twelve-bar blues form originated in jazz and has always been prevalent in jazz performance. The most important characteristic of jazz, however, is improvisation. Virtually every jazz selection will focus on improvisation, even when many other characteristics remain optional. Jazz continues to develop, absorb new styles and techniques, and change with great rapidity, but improvisation, the blues, and the vigorous pulse remain reasonably constant throughout its history of development from folk music to art music.

Jazz historians have frequently mentioned the lifestyles of famous jazz personalities, especially their racial problems, commercial success, poverty, drugs, marital problems, and associations with prostitution and the underworld. Unquestionably such material may be of interest to the general reader. On the other hand, much of it is beside the point, some of it is subject to distortion, and most of it is no one's business but the performer's. The performer's private life may have influenced his music in some significant way, but most of the time such notions are pure conjecture. Usually we learn more about the artist from being told of his musical influences and training, or to what records he listened often, or of the statements he made about his craft.

The real history of jazz is in the music itself, especially in the solos of such great improvisers as Louis Armstrong, Coleman Hawkins, Lester Young, Charles Parker, Miles Davis, and John Coltrane. Ironically, it is the long improvised solos, with all their complexities, that have widened the gulf between the jazz performer and his audience in recent years. When single records were still recorded at 78 RPM, whole selections were only three to four minutes long. If it required one minute to play the melody at the beginning and another minute to the play the melody at the end, then the listener faced only one or two minutes of improvisation between the more understandable melodic segments. But an average selection today might be more like Freddie Hubbard's "Mr.

Clean," which is thirteen and one half minutes long. With one minute of melody at the beginning and one again at the end, we are given eleven and one half minutes of improvisation to enjoy, decipher, or endure, as the case may be. From a purely musical point of view, the longer selections made possible by the long-playing record (lp) did much to further jazz as an art form, by providing more time for the natural unfolding of solo material. From the audience's point of view, longer selections posed greater challenges, causing some to give up trying to understand, remember, and enjoy the music. We can't turn back the clock or hold back the progress of music and recording technology, but we can make an effort to reach a deeper understanding of what transpires in a jazz performance, in particular in the creative core of jazz, the improvised solo.

SUGGESTED LISTENING

In the definition of the word *jazz,* many elements and influences were mentioned that especially pertain to early jazz; these should be aurally experienced by the reader. The same definition mentioned the "development from folk music to art music," which should also be experienced. Therefore, it is suggested that the reader could benefit from a very abbreviated history of jazz in sound. The Smithsonian Collection of Jazz (mentioned in the author's Preface and referred to in listings as SC) will be used whenever possible, to avoid sending the reader on an almost assuredly futile mission to locate the recordings in their original form.

Era/style	Title	Artist/Group	Recording Data
Ragtime	"Maple Leaf Rag"	Scott Joplin	SC, side 1 track 1
Blues	"Lost Your Head Blues"	Bessie Smith	SC, side 1, track 5
Dixieland	"Black Bottom Stomp"	Jelly Roll Morton	SC, side 2, track 1

Era/style	Title	Artist/Group	Recording Data
Swing	"Lunceford Special"	Jimmy Lunceford	SC, side 5, track 3
Be-Bop	"Shaw 'Nuff"	Dizzy Gillespie	SC, side 7, track 6
Modern	"D.B.B."	Brecker Brothers	Arista AL 4037

Later in our discussion, six performers were listed as great improvising soloists. Listening to the following list of selections would help confirm their greatness in the reader's mind.

Improviser	Title	Recording Data
Louis Armstrong	"S.O.L. Blues"	SC, side 2, track 6
Coleman Hawkins	"Body and Soul"	SC, side 4, track 4
Lester Young	"Lester Leaps In"	SC, side 6, track 1
Charles Parker	"Koko"	SC, side 7, track 7
Miles Davis	"So What"	SC, side 11, track 3
John Coltrane	"Pursuance"	Impulse A-77

Two further selections are suggested because they relate to the comparison between the long-playing record ("Mr. Clean") and its predecessor, the 78 RPM single.

Group	Title	Recording Data
Freddie Hubbard	"Mr. Clean"	CTI 6007
Miles Davis	"Boplicity"	SC, side 9, track 1

2

FORMAL STRUCTURES IN JAZZ

THE VEHICLE

Virtually all jazz selections are based on some sort of tune or song. Whether a well-known standard or a recently composed original, it is a tune nonetheless. The design of the tune will be present during the improvised solos as well as during the playing of the melody (usually at the beginning and again at the end of the selection). The word *tune* here refers chiefly to a melody with its accompanying chords. If there are words to the tune, they are likely to occur (if at all) during the playing of the melody. Furthermore, the words are seldom known or contemplated by the improvising soloists. An exception to the rule was tenor saxophonist Lester Young, included with the suggested listening of Chapter 1 ("Lester Leaps In"). Young was once quoted as saying that he didn't like to improvise on a tune to which he didn't know the words. He went on to say that he heard the words in his mind as he improvised. There is evidence to suggest that the cur-

7

rent generation of jazz musicians considers the words and
subject matter of the tune more than did their predecessors,
but such practice is still rare.

A tune will also have rhythms, but like words the
rhythms will be more structured and apparent during the
playing of the melody than during the improvisation on it.
Again, contemporary jazz tunes are more likely to use repetitive rhythmic patterns as an important aspect of the tune,
even during the improvisations. Herbie Hancock's "Maiden
Voyage"[1] is a good example of a jazz performance in which
the rhythmic feeling of the melody chorus is strongly
suggested throughout the selection. The majority of jazz
selections still tend to be without the structured rhythms of
the melody section, once the improvisation begins.

Although the melody is almost synonymous with the
tune itself and therefore included with the accompanying
chords as an important structural element of the tune, it is
also true that even the melody will seldom be present during
the improvisations. The earliest jazz players based their improvisations on the melody, and once again, contemporary
players are apparently giving more thought to retaining at
least portions of the melody in their improvisations; but the
great majority of jazz performances won't include such practice. It should be pointed out here that improvisations also
have melodies and rhythms, but except in rare instances the
improvised melodies and rhythms won't be symmetrically
structured in terms of the sort of repetitions used during the
playing of the tune's melody.

To sum up, tunes have a melody, accompanying chords,
rhythm, and words. The real identity of the tune, for most
jazz players anyway, is the sequence used in the accompanying chords, as the improvising soloist generally does not base
his solo on the melody, rhythms, or words. We can, however,
take note of the fact that contemporary players are beginning to explore those areas.

[1]"Maiden Voyage," Herbie Hancock, Blue Note 84195.

The sequence of chords used to accompany the melody is generally referred to as the *chord progression* or the *chord changes,* or simply *progression* or *changes* in the vernacular. The chord progression to the tune is usually retained with exactness *throughout* the selection, even during the improvised solos, simply by repeating the entire progression (which will be the same length each time through as it was in accompanying one entire playing of the melody) over and over.

The term *vehicle* was first applied in jazz by Dizzy Gillespie as a near-synonym of *tune*, describing the improviser's use of a tune as a sort of machine on which he rides during his improvisation. No doubt Gillespie used the term as part of his humor, poking fun at those who would introduce jazz selections as though trying to sanctify the proceedings. But *vehicle,* nonetheless, describes the situation about as well as any word could.

THE CHORUS

One complete playing of the melody, or one complete playing of the chord progression, would be one *chorus.* One chorus of our national anthem would encompass "O, say, can you see" to "the home of the brave." But as anthems generally are not of the more repetitious form of most tunes used by improvisers, the following lyric (words) by Torme and Wells will better serve as an example of the chorus structure and its subdivisions:

THE CHRISTMAS SONG

A Chestnuts roasting on an open fire,
Jack Frost nipping at your nose.
Yuletide carols being sung by a choir, and
Folks dressed up like eskimos. Everybody

Knows a turkey and some mistletoe,
A   Help to make the season bright.
Tiny tots with their eyes all aglow,
Will find it hard to sleep tonight.

They know that Santa's on his way;
B   He's loaded lots of toys and goodies on his sleigh.
And every mother's child is gonna' spy,
To see if reindeer really know how to fly.

And so, I'm offering this simple phrase,
A   To kids from one to ninety-two.
Although it's been said many times, 'many ways,
Merry Christmas to you.

There are sixteen lines in all, each line taking two measures to be sung. The music (melody and progression) is organized into eight-measure phrases (or four lines of the lyric), three of which are nearly identical (labeled *A*), with the other a contrasting section (*B*).

Specifically, what is meant by an eight-measure phrase in the melody and chord progression is that after four lines of words, the melody becomes as it was at the beginning, and so do the chords. The sets of words "Chestnuts roasting on an open fire" and "Knows a turkey and some mistletoe" each begin an eight-measure phrase that will use essentially the same melody and chord progression, although the last two measures (or the fourth line of words in each of the first two four-line groups) are slightly different. The last four-line segment, beginning with "And so, I'm offering this simple phrase," uses the same melody and chord progression over its eight-bar phrase. Hence, all three of those segments are labeled *A* for purposes of analysis. The melody and chords are very different in the *B* section, offering a contrast to the first two *A* sections that makes it easier to repeat the *A* section one more time after *B*. The contrasting section (*B*) is commonly called the *bridge* or the *channel*. In summation, we have a tune that can be subdivided into four eight-measure phrases, which because of their similarity or dissimilarity could be thought of as of the form AABA. Played through once, that AABA pattern would make up one *chorus*.

It should be mentioned here that the word *chorus* is sometimes applied as a synonym for *solo*, which could be confusing because a solo may contain one or many choruses of the variety we've just described. If you hear someone say something like, "That was a beautiful chorus you played," understand that he may be referring to a multiple-chorus solo (which is very common).

It's extremely difficult to be sure that any two people, let alone an even greater number, will know the same tunes. "Christmas Song" was chosen because, being a seasonal song, it is likely to be known by many readers. Furthermore, it was written by a jazz singer (Mel Torme) and is structured much like a jazz ballad. If "Christmas Song" is not familiar, "The Girl From Ipanema" and "I Got Rhythm" also have an AABA form.

Although the AABA form is extremely prevalent among jazz vehicles, there are others. The ABAB and ABAC forms are also common, appearing in tunes like "Moon River," "Someday My Prince Will Come," "Stardust," and "Foggy Day." I am avoiding mention of jazz originals becuase of their possible unfamiliarity to the reader, but many of the jazz originals also use AABA or ABAB forms, or virtually any other formal structure used in a popular tune.

CHORD PROGRESSIONS

Without going into technical evidence, it should be obvious to anyone who listens to a reasonable quantity of music that many chord progressions sound alike or similar to one another. The average chord progression is likely to contain only one or two (if any) chords that will be genuine surprises to the ear.[2] Chords usually move in patterns or sequences that are relatively easy to assimilate, even anticipate, with the ear. This holds true for the nontechnical listener as well.

It is suggested that the reader try counting measures[3] and "measure groups" while listening to the opening melody chorus of a jazz selection. Learn to recognize identical or nearly identical measure groups (usually eight-measure groupings), and try to decipher the form in terms of patterns such as AABA or ABAB.

Continue counting and identifying segments of the tune during the improvisation, especially the beginning of a new chorus (if the improviser plays more than one chorus in his solo). Sometimes you'll hear the player improvise a phrase that begins before the end of one chorus and is completed in the early portion of the next chorus (a variation called *over-lapping*). Other times you may be able to detect that the soloist is winding down or tapering to a close that can be closely pinpointed and anticipated if you've kept count of the measure groups. The next soloist will generally begin his solo at the crossroads between one chorus and another.

The number of chords in the progressions to different tunes may vary sharply. Hubbard's "Mr. Clean" has but one chord in its progression, whereas Coltrane's "Giant Steps"[4] has fifty-two chords. Most tunes will contain about twenty-four chords (counting the repeated phrases), moving at the pace of a new chord every one or two measures. Most tunes will be about thirty-two measures long, like "Christmas Song." "Maiden Voyage" has only eight chord changes, yet it is thirty-two measures in length, as each chord lasts for four measures.

---

[2] A thorough analysis and comparison of eighty-three chord progressions appears in *Improvising Jazz*, Coker, Prentice-Hall, Englewood Cliffs, 1964.

[3] The grouping together of beats. For example, in the very common 4/4 time signature, four beats will equal one measure.

[4] "Giant Steps," John Coltrane, Atlantic SD-1311.

Another helpful exercise for the reader would be to hum or hear internally the tune's melody along with the improvised sections, keeping pace with the tempo, measures, and phrases. Some improvisers admit to inwardly hearing the melody while they are improvising, to aid them in keeping their place in the tune. This practice is especially prevalent among players who don't know the chord progression well enough, but it is occasionally practiced by those who are theoretically knowledgeable.

As final evidence of the jazz player's use of the chord progression, consider that even in the thirties players, like Coleman Hawkins on "Body And Soul," were recording tunes, even ballads, in which their solos seldom contained even a hint of the given melody. Or that in the forties, players like Dizzy Gillespie and Charles Parker not only abandoned the given melody in their solos but often omitted even the initial melody chorus or wrote a new melody for the opening and closing choruses, using the chord progression of an already existing tune. Some examples of this mild form of plagiarism (you can't copyright a chord progression) are:

Standard Tune	becomes:	*Be-Bop Tune*
"Cherokee		"Koko"
"What Is This Thing Called Love?"		"Hot House"
"Whispering"		"Groovin' High"
"Back Home Again in Indiana"		"Donna Lee"
"Sweet Georgia Brown"		"Dig"

It's easy to see why jazz declined so in mass popularity around the time of Gillespie and Parker. Despite their gift, the music was being carried swiftly along a path away from its folk-like beginnings and toward an art music that would have a dedicated but much smaller audience than before. Those who had hopes of hearing a familiar melody and sound were doomed to be disappointed.

It is interesting to notice that the next musical craze was rock and roll music, arriving in the fifties, which also developed at so swift a pace that, by the late sixties, rock fans began turning away as had the jazz fans of the forties, bewildered by the artistic sophistication of what had been their music just a few years prior to that. As there was a Dixieland revival in 1948, there were rock and roll revivals in the late sixties, attended by those who liked the music better before the complexities set in. In either case, jazz or rock, the styles have evolved into a music that is well worth the effort to understand.

SUGGESTED LISTENING

Listen to Herbie Hancock's "Maiden Voyage" (Blue Note 84195) at least several times, as it has been previously cited as:

1. a jazz performance that examplifies the somewhat scarce practice of retaining the rhythmic style that accompanies the melody-playing choruses, even during the improvised solos; and

2. a tune that has the usual length of thirty-two measures, but in which there are but eight changes of chord, because of the unusually long (four measures) duration assigned to each chord.

It is suggested that one listening be devoted to the unique and seemingly asymmetrically placed accents in the background rhythms that accompany the very sparse melody. Notice that those rhythms are suggested throughout the performance, in a more subtle manner, even behind the solos.

On a second listening, count the thirty-two measures of each complete chorus, noticing their subdivision into eight-measure segments, a pattern especially noticeable during the melody choruses. Also, notice the four-measure durations of each chord. If your count always comes out at tiwce the number, you are counting at twice the actual tempo, though some of the sounds being made are at twice the tempo. On the other hand, if your count always is half the given number, then of course you are counting at one half the actual tempo. This is commonly referred to as *half-time* or *In 2*. When the feeling of the music is twice the known tempo, the resulting effect is referred to as *double-time*.

Finally, listen again and follow the form of the tune, which will be found to be an AABA structure. If you have never heard the recording before, listen to it regularly for a while, in a more generally appreciative, relaxed manner. In other words, get to know the record so that it can be heard internally, in the memory. It is a significant recording of recent jazz history, with far-reaching influence.

Listen to Don Byas recording of "I Got Rhythm" (side 7, track 4 in the Smithsonian Collection). Here it is played as a thirty-two measure tune, though the tune in its original state used a two-measure *tag* (extension) at the end of each chorus, totalling thirty-four. For example, Benny Goodman's recording of the same tune used the tag on each chorus, even the improvised ones, which makes for more difficulty in counting the resulting ten-measure *A* section at the end of each chorus. (This is a good example of an instance in which it would be helpful to hear the melody internally while improvising). After checking the thirty-two measure length, the eight-measure subdivisions, and the AABA form, try singing the melody against all ensuing choruses after the melody chorus. It's not easy to do, as it is necessary at first to avoid being distracted by all the improvisation, but during the successful moments of the practice, definite benefits will be derived.

Then listen again to Gillespie's "Shaw 'Nuff" (side 7, track 6), a be-bop tune that uses the chord progression of "I Got Rhythm" (also a thirty-two measure version). Although the melody is different in the be-bop version, it still follows the AABA structure, melodically and harmonically. You should be alerted to the fact that "Shaw 'Nuff" has a long introduction before the repetitious AABA choruses begin. After the rhythm section plays eight measures and is followed by sixteen bars played by the horns, the AABA choruses may be counted. In counting a fast tempo such as this, it might be advisable to count in half-time, or in two long beats per measure, in order not to twist the tongue and/or lose one's place in the tune. Measures may also be counted in an even longer beat by counting only the first beat of each four-beat measure. In this fashion, it becomes possible to count, say, an eight-measure segment, as "one-two-three-four-five-six-seven-eight" instead of "one-one-one-one-one-one-one-one." Jazz musicians learn to count or sense two-, four-, and eight-measure segments, rather than beats or single measures. Feeling the music in longer segments encourages the graceful flow of the improvised melodic phrases. Try to sing "I Got Rhythm" against the melody of "Shaw 'Nuff" (without forgetting the twenty-four measure introduction), then against the improvised choruses, as well. How many choruses does each soloist take? How many choruses comprise the Don Byas and Slam Stewart (bassist on the Byas version of "I Got Rhythm") solos: Begin to notice chorus structures (AABA, ABAB, etc.) on everything to which you listen, as well as noting how many choruses each soloist uses in this improvisation.

Listen again to "Koko" (side 7, track 7), this time to hear an AABA tune that lasts for sixty-four measures per chorus, subdivided into sixteen-measure segments. How many choruses does Parker use in his solo? (His solo begins after another long introduction, this time thirty-two measures long, without being followed by the usual opening melody chorus.) The third sixteen-measure segment is the *B* section. Notice the interesting chords and keys encountered in that bridge. "Koko" uses the chord progression of an earlier standard tune called "Cherokee," popularized on record by

the Charlie Barnet Orchestra. If you know the melody to "Cherokee," try humming or singing that melody against "Koko."

If you were successful in locating a copy of Hubbard's recording of "Mr. Clean," you should listen to it again, noting this time the sound and feeling of a tune that has only one chord in its progression, and also to count measures. The melody lasts sixteen measures and is then played again (repeated), the end of each sixteen-bar phrase being marked by a break in the pulse, when the entire ensemble plays a rather complicated melody together. This part of the melody is called a *break* (sometimes a *solo break,* when improvised by a soloist), because of the interruption of pulse-keeping and accompaniment sounds in general. Such breaks are counted, in terms of measures, and are a part of the tune's duration. Note that the break is played, apart from the remainder of the melody, at the close of each solo. Its placement should be at the end (last four measures) of a sixteen-measure segment. Count measures during the seemingly unstructured form of the solos (which might sound unstructured because there is an absence of chord changes, in the usual sense) to see if there are sixteen-measure phrases being observed. Note whether the break begins on the thirteenth measure of a sixteen-measure phrase, when the break is used by itself as an interlude between soloists.

Listen to John Coltrane's "Giant Steps" (Atlantic SD-1311), which has a fast tempo, a slow-moving ABAB melody, and a fast-moving chord progression. The rhythmic motion of changing chords (as their durations will vary) is called *harmonic rhythm.* "Giant Steps" is a rare example of a tune whose harmonic rhythm is identical to the rhythm of the melody. That is, each time a new melody note appears, a new chord arrives simultaneously. As most of the chords in "Giant Steps" last only two beats each, there are, in contrast to "Mr. Clean," many more chord changes (a faster harmonic rhythm). Because the melody is sparse and easy to memorize, and agrees with the harmonic rhythm, it will be easy for you to know for a certainty where the chords are changing. Assimilate the sound of a tune with many chords, like "Giant Steps" and compare it with a polar opposite, "Mr. Clean."

Finally, to better appreciate the Coleman Hawkins solo on "Body And Soul" (SC, side 4, track 4), first locate and listen to a simple, sung version of the same tune by another artist until you can inwardly hear the whole *AABA* tune in its traditional setting. Then listen again to the Hawkins version and try to hear the melody against his improvisation, which begins immediately after the four-measure introduction by the piano. Note that but the merest suggestions of the melody appear throughout the two-chorus solo.

3

THE RHYTHM SECTION

The term *rhythm section* probably began to be used in the early days of the big jazz bands (1925-1930), when one spoke of the trumpet section, the trombone section, or the saxophone section, in other words, when there was, for the first time in jazz, multiplicity of the trumpet, trombone, and saxophone (or clarinet). In prior times, as in the New Orleans style (1890-1925), such instruments seldom appeared in numbers greater than one. But when one spoke of the remaining instruments of the big band, like the piano, guitar, bass, and drums, the term *rhythm section* was used, lumping together four rather dissimilar instruments that shared the common function of maintaining the pulse or beat for some eight to thirteen wind instruments, in ensemble and during solos. This is an oversimplification, of course, as their duties also included supplying chords, bass lines, solos, rhythmic settings, and even melodies. But jazz is a music "with the big beat" or an emphasized pulse, and the piano, guitar, bass, and drums are especially suited to carrying that beat.

It is probably true, however, that the name *rhythm section* is, when applied to today's jazz, inaccurate and degrading. The term reduces those four marvelous instruments to the function of a bass drum player in a marching band or a drone in Eastern music. We surely wouldn't refer to the Oscar Peterson Trio or the Bill Evans Trio (each made up of piano, bass, and drums) as a rhythm section, as each of these trios is an entire group, one that does not rely on wind instruments to carry melody, harmony, arrangement, or solos.

Most music of the Western world will be found to have three main structural elements: bass line, chords, and melody. In the Baroque trio of the seventeenth century, for example, the bass line was played by a viola da gamba, the chords by a harpsichord, and the melody by a wind instrument (flute, recorder, etc.) or perhaps a violin. A group of instruments like piano, guitar, bass, and drums can easily carry the three structural elements of bass line, chords, and melody (indeed all three elements could be carried by piano or guitar alone), plus the added rhythmic dimension made possible by the inclusion of drums. Doubtless, we will continue to refer to them as a *rhythm section* for some time, but we mustn't think of that section as existing merely to supply a "big beat."

Such misconceptions have even found their way into the minds of the musicians themselves. For example, an arranger is subject to scoring all the horn parts first, leaving the rhythm section parts for the last, sometimes not even supplying written parts for them, an omission he could hardly consider in the case of, say, the lead trumpet part. For another example, the pecking order for improvised solos in sessions and in recordings will usually direct that all the wind instruments play their solos first, giving the last (and usually shorter) solos to the members of the rhythm section, when some of their solo drive has been dampened or used up accompanying long solos by the wind instruments. Rhythm section players, then, are understandably reluctant to come to a jam session and receive more punishment, especially if there are too many horn players (as, remember, the rhythm section plays virtually all the time, regardless of who is soloing). Still another example of warped values is evident in some horn players who won't learn the chord progressions by hard work and study, but expect the guitarist, pianist, and bass player to know the progressions and supply them endlessly while the horn player tries to find his notes by ear and guesswork. It would be helpful to take a closer look at each of the instruments of the rhythm section and how they function in the jazz group.

DRUMS

It has often been stated by jazz historians that jazz rhythms have their origins in the music of West Africa. No doubt there is some truth in this, but it would be a mistake to think that jazz rhythms and West African rhythms are very much alike. The music of West Africa is far more sophisticated and complex by comparison and well beyond the grasp of jazz drummers, even black drummers, as their color and ancestry cannot overcome several centuries of detachment from African culture. Even the music played at Congo Square in New Orleans by the blacks who gathered there in the late nineteenth century was already a diluted form of West African music, and the unusual rhythm instruments used there were largely at variance with the instruments of West Africa. Whatever similarities did exist during the spawning of jazz, soon faded away, replaced by a forerunner of the modern drum set (bass drum, snare drum, tom-toms, and cymbals). One of the earliest jazz drummers was Baby Dodds, but except for very small details, we can hardly relate his style to the West African style. In fact, we'd have an easier time proving that jazz elements like improvisation, call and response patterns, the blues style, jazz intonation, and jazz phrasing are derived from the West African culture. About all that remains of African drumming in jazz (recent efforts to rediscover African drumming notwithstanding) is the general emphasis on rhythm and a few polymetric aspects.[1]

Early jazz drummers (1900-1930) were not very prominent or adventurous, tending to play relatively simple time-keeping figures and seldom soloing. Ironically, white drummer Gene Krupa probably did more to liberate the drummer from purely time-keeping functions than any drummer before him. This can be easily recognized by comparing Krupa's recordings (with Benny Goodman in the late thirties) with previous drummers. He is significantly prominent and solos often in those recordings. There were other important drummers in Krupa's time, like Sonny Greer (with Duke Ellington) and Cozy Cole, but Krupa's extraversion and flashiness were needed to bring the drums out of the purely supporting role. He forced you to listen to the drummer. He played a loud, heavy pulse with his bass drum, pounded out a quasi-jungle style on tom-toms (which was purely illusory and bore little resemblance to West African drumming), participated heavily on the overall sound of the ensemble, and played virtuosic, dramatic solos.

Joe Jones was another important drummer, also active in the late thirties, with the Count Basie Orchestra. Rather than focusing on a solo style, as Krupa did, Jones mastered the rhythm-section function of the drummer, supplying a solid, steady beat and blending with the other members of that great rhythm section (Basie on piano, Freddie Green on guitar and Walter Page on bass).

A few years later, in the early forties, the be-bop style was born. As it was a very different style from the music of the Swing Era (1930–1940), it required a vastly different approach to playing drums, which was first supplied by Kenny Clarke. Clarke did away with the bass drum pulse, keeping time on the cymbals instead, using the bass drum only for explosive accents or for echoing improvised figures played

[1] Polymetric means the playing of one time signature against another.

on the snare drum. The pulse was infinitely more subtle than Krupa's, replacing the bass drum's *"thump-thump-thump-thump"* with a "ding, *ding*-a, ding, *ding*-a" on a very large cymbal (italics are used to show accents here).

Another change took place in the pulse feeling: whereas previous drummers either accented all four beats of a measure (as in 4/4 time) or accented the first and third beats, Clarke and other bop drummers switched the accents to the second and fourth beats, playing them on the sock cymbals (two cymbals that come together, operated by the foot) in a figure and sound that might be described as "(rest), *chick*, (rest), *chick*." Note that both the sock cymbal figure and the large (*ride*) cymbal figure played by Clarke have accents on the second and fourth beats and that neither figure is merely a thumping, unadorned pulse beat. The sock cymbal figure omits the first and third beats altogether and the ride cymbal figure adds sound between the beats, represented here by the "a" of "*ding*-a." These changes made quite a difference in the overall sound of drummers, the pulse, and the rhythm section.

Another innovation of the Be-bop Era (chiefly 1945–50) was the new relationship between drummer and ensemble, particularly in the big bands. In the late forties, Woody Herman recorded "The Goof And I," in which drummer Don Lamond was very prominent, not as a soloist but as a sort of rhythmic coach to the entire ensemble. Lamond emphasized the ensemble's heavier accents, duplicating them on his bass drum, sometimes on snare drum or cymbals as well. This is not to be confused with the thumping *pulse-beat* played by Krupa in an earlier time. In Lamond's playing the bass drum was only supporting the band's accents, which are much less frequent than the pulse. His bass drum sound was explosively loud by contrast with the beats in which he wasn't using the bass drum at all. Lamond also played loud figures just prior to ensemble entrances and accents that made it easier for the ensemble to feel their rhythmic figures accurately. Several new terms were coined in this period; (1) *bomb,* a name for the explosive accents; (2) *set-up*, a figure that preceded an ensemble entrance and made that entrance more positive and accurate; and (3) *fill*, material improvised by the drummer in otherwise empty places, to take up the slack.

During and after the Be-Bop Era, the drums became an instrument for sizzling virtuosos, especially in the hands of Max Roach, whose phenomenal technique was baffling to the drummers of the time. Roach was particularly dazzling both as a soloist and as a drummer who could drive a group through some of the fastest tempos ever attempted by a jazz group. Most of his career was spent playing in the greatest of the small groups of that period, with Charles Parker, Dizzy Gillespie, Sonny Rollins, and the Max Roach–Clifford Brown Quintet. Roach dwelt on polymetric figures and on rhythmic form (variations on rhythmic motives).[2]

In the early fifties, while the Max Roach–Clifford Brown Quintet was in full bloom, a group in Detroit let by Barry Harris was featuring a new drummer on the rise, Elvin Jones, who later joined the John Coltrane Quartet and made some of the most significant recordings of the late fifties and early sixties with this group, including the album *A Love Supreme*. Jones perfectly complemented the dynamic Coltrane style. Far from merely keeping time for the group, Jones was a fully participating member, coinciding with and echoing every important rhythmic nuance of both the ensemble and the solos. It was a boiling, brewing, conversational style that didn't wait for empty spots to be filled.

About this time musicians and critics were beginning to refer to a new rhythmic concept, called the *implied beat,* in which it was no longer necessary for the rhythm section, particularly the drummer, to produce timekeeping figures. Instead, as long as they were all feeling the pulse together (and they were), it was no longer necessary to play the pulse

[2]Sometimes the rhythmic motives used by Roach were actually the rhythms of a known melody. By using the various components of his drum set, he even implied the *contours* of the melody.

itself, as it would be apparent anyway in everything they chose to play. In other words, they didn't ignore the pulse, as everything was related to and measured by that pulse, but they simply didn't need to thump it out anymore. The pulse would be implied by what they did play. This was new to jazz, yet it had existed in many other forms of music for centuries. Thus we seem now to have arrived at a point about 180 degrees from where we started our discussion, at a stage where pulse-keeping was deemed redundant.

Compared to singers and to players of wind instruments and strings, a drummer plays an instrument that is almost without the capability of being tonal or melodic. Early drummers in jazz, when they tightened or loosened the heads on their drums, doubtlessly were more attentive to the *tone quality* than to the actual *pitch* of each of the drums. And the drummer is not likely to change the tuning of the drums to suit the key of each selection played. Furthermore, the pitches produced by drums do not sustain, nor are they very distinct vibrationally or a high enough range to be perceived as specific pitches by many listeners. Even the cymbals, for all their beautiful ringing, are almost indistinct in terms of specific pitches heard by the average listener. Finally, the cymbals and drums used in jazz are, under normal circumstances, not built for the *spontaneous* tuning to specific pitches during the performance used with the timpani (which can be spontaneously tuned, owing to a foot-pedal mechanism) or the tabla (of India, tuned by pressing on the bottom head of the drum with the hand that is not beating the rhythm). Drummers like Art Blakey partially solved the problem by pressing the top head of the drum with an elbow, thereby raising and lowering the pitch at will. This limited solution, however, could not, in itself, push the drum style much closer to a recognizable melody.

If drums are relatively unmelodic, compared to wind and string instruments, they are even less capable of producing harmony. Thanks to these limitations, drummers often acquire, by experience, a defensive attitude about studying music, formally. Melody and harmony reign supreme in music classes (too much so, in fact), but the members of the class who play drums have less opportunity to apply melodic and harmonic principles to their instrument. Application and experience being crucial to the assimilation of such principles, the drummer is often at a disadvantage and called a "slow learner."

The solutions to all these problems are interesting to observe, historically. Krupa was already working on the melodic problem in the thirties, by rapid alternation between the different drums, creating the illusion of counterpoint (simultaneous melodic–rhythmic events, usually in imitation), and by using accessories, like the cowbell or the woodblock, in semi-melodic ways. Drummers of the forties, like Max Roach and Shelly Manne, began tuning their drums to specific pitches to aid the drive toward a more melodic concept. Roach and Mel Lewis did much to aid the element of story-telling form to the drum solo, that is, they repeated rhythmic motives and developed them slowly and completely, like the melodies to familiar songs. Some drummers, like Benny Barth, spent many practice hours drumming the rhythms of hundreds of popular and standard songs, in an effort to be more melodic.

Somewhere along the way, drummers stopped trying to compete melodically with the other instruments. Instead, they developed a pride in *percussive* melodies, not compared to or in strict imitation of or limited by standard pitch–melody concepts. Listen, for example, to the constantly chattering, conversational style of Elvin Jones, both in soloing and in accompanimental capacities.

Many of the foregoing contributions came together in the drum playing of Tony Williams, in the sixties and into the present, and were developed further by him. Finally, spontaneous tuning of pitches was added (though not in imitation of traditional scales and melodies), chiefly by Billy Cobham, through the use of electronic gadgetry that can alter pitch, quality, and reverberation. A Cobham solo is, by anyone's standards, extremely melodic.

Even the overall image of the drummer's musicianship has increased greatly over the years. In the forties and early fifties, drummers like Tiny Kahn and Louie Bellson were writing choice arrangements and teaching chord progressions to other members of a jam session. In 1958, at the Monterey Jazz Festival, Max Roach electrified the San Francisco Symphony with his performance of a difficult piece by Peter Phillips, written for Roach and the orchestra. By the end of the sixties, Elvin Jones and Tony Williams had become leaders of major jazz combos. In the late sixties, Stan Kenton had two drummers who had switched from wind instruments to drums, Dee Barton and John von Olen. And then there are those, like Stevie Wonder and Billy Cobham, who can perform virtually every task of the well-rounded musician, composing, arranging, playing several instruments, singing, and leading, with success and with perfection. Drummers like Alan Dawson and Max Roach, in addition to being great players, have also become successful as teachers of jazz drums in major colleges and conservatories.

Another dimension was added to drumming in the late sixties when Miles Davis added a *percussionist* to his rock-oriented jazz group that recorded albums like *In A Silent Way* and *Bitches Brew*. Davis retained the drummer, as well, simply adding Jim Riley or Airto Moreira on miscellaneous percussion instruments too numerous to list fully, but the numbers included strings of bells, Latin American rhythm instruments, and virtually anything that would rattle, scrape, or jingle. The percussionist's music (written) or parts were generally unassigned, leaving to their tasteful discretion to play whatever and whenever they felt the need. Such percussionists add color, texture, and dimension to the overall sound of the group. In a sense, we have returned to percussion instruments like those used in Congo Square, a full 360 degrees of change and development.

BASS

Although the bass seems in most jazz groups to be the heartbeat of the group, as well as the instrument best suited to carrying a bass line, the earliest jazz groups were apt to be without a string bass or to use a bass horn or tuba instead. In fact, it was quite common in the twenties and early thirties for the bass player to carry along a bass horn as well as the string bass to play on some selections. Even when the string bass became a more standard instrument in the jazz bands, its role was subdued and restricted to playing simple chord tones on the first and third beats of the measure most of the time, and he seldom, if ever, played a solo.

The liberator of the bass was Jimmy Blanton, bassist with Duke Ellington in 1940–41, who is credited with creating the *walking bass line*[3] as well as producing some of the first melodic bass solos. He died very young, before his full potential was realized. Ellington recorded an album with Blanton that illustrates his great talent. In its 10″ lp form of the fifties (already a reissue of the 78 RPM originals), the album was called "Duos." His lead was taken by bassists of the forties, like Oscar Pettiford, Milt Hinton, Slam Stewart (who bowed his solos and hummed in unison with himself), and Curley Russell. Pettiford's impressive technique and hornlike melodic style was followed by several bass virtuosos of the fifties and sixties, like Charles Mingus, Paul Chambers (with Miles Davis), and the astoundingly swift and complex style of Scotty LaFaro. It was most unfortunate that the lives of Blanton, Pettiford, Chambers, and LaFaro were all cut short, at the height of their playing careers. Another important bassist Ray Brown, is a master of the walking bass line, playing with one of the biggest sounds possible to achieve. He played with Dizzy Gillespie and, later, with the original Modern Jazz

---

[3] A bass line, generally in quarter notes (one note for each beat), that moves in a scalar, semi-chromatic fashion, as opposed to two notes per measure on simple chord tones.

Quartet (before Percy Heath).[4] He then joined the Oscar Peterson Trio, beginning a long and productive association. Percy Heath is an uncommonly well-schooled bassist, having spent most of his career with the Modern Jazz Quartet. For the last decade, the giants of the bass have been Ron Carter (with Miles Davis) and Jimmy Garrison (who gained fame with the John Coltrane Quartet). Garrison, probably inspired by Mingus and Brown, was largely responsible for the use of double-stops (playing of more than one note simultaneously) in bass solos. Another strong contributor to the bass style is Charlie Haden, who is most often heard with Ornette Coleman's Quartet.

When the rock style began to permeate jazz music, many bassists switched from the acoustic bass (wooden, upright) to the electric bass. Most of them, like Ron Carter, continue to play both acoustic and electric basses. Probably no bassist today rivals Stanley Clarke (with Chick Corea) in his handling of both kinds of bass, perfectly accommodating the jazz and rock styles.

A stunning new arrival on the jazz scene is bassist Joco Pastorius (with Herbie Hancock and Weather Report), whose remarkable speed, mastery of double-stops (actually many are full, rich *chords*), command of the *harmonic*[5] range, and tasteful use of electronic gadgetry when needed has made him an overnight sensation. On "Portrait Of Tracy" (Epic PE 33949) he plays the piece unaccompanied, supplying melody, chords, and bass line, making his bass sound much like an electric piano. His improvisations, which move as quickly and gracefully as solos heard on any other instrument, are highly original and filled with choice melodies. Pastorius also composes and arranges music with a talent comparable to his performing level.

[4]The first jazz concert chamber group.

[5]*Harmonics* are achieved on stringed instruments by very lightly touching the strings at certain places (while plucking with the other hand, of course), causing the pitches to be much higher but related to the pitch that would have been produced had the string been depressed all the way, as it normally is.

The bass has undergone quite a transformation. Like the drums, the bass was relatively insignificant at first, sometimes not even included in the earlier jazz groups, and the first assignments were pretty mundane. People like Blanton, Pettiford, Mingus, and LaFaro proved the instrument's virtuoso possibilities and soloing capacity, while Clarke and Pastorius have brought the instrument to its full fruition, technically and stylistically.

GUITAR

The earliest jazz guitarists were mostly blues singers, like Huddy Ledbetter ("Leadbelly"), who used the guitar in an almost purely accompanimental capacity. In fact, a banjo was the instrument more likely to be found in the early jazz groups. Banjoist Johnny St. Cyr was a regular member of the famous Joe "King" Oliver and Louis Armstrong Orchestras in the early and middle twenties. In time the banjo was replaced by the guitar; for a while, at least, the guitar's role in the group was somewhat limited, like those of the bass and drums. The early guitars were not amplified, played virtually no solos, and simply supplied a strumming, pulse-keeping part. Eddie Lang (with Red Nichols, Miff Mole, Joe Venuti, and other Dixieland groups of the late twenties and the thirties) was one of the first liberators of the guitar, playing solos occasionally and having a more important role to play in the rhythm section.

Charlie Christian was one of the most significant and widely imitated guitarists in jazz history. It is remarkable that Christian lived for only two years after being discovered by Benny Goodman. Although he died at the age of twenty-three, his influence has been felt by nearly every major guitarist since that time. Furthermore, Christian was simultaneously involved in two different eras of jazz history: the

Swing Era (the period that was noted for the profusion of famous big bands and the jitterbug dancers) and the Be-Bop Era that followed. Christian's guitar was amplified electronically, and he was a heavily featured soloist. His improvising style was angular (that is, his improvised melodies contained many wide leaps) and extremely original, seemingly without precedent, though Christian claimed that Gypsy guitarist Django Reinhardt was a strong influence for him.

After Christian, the guitar became a much more popular jazz instrument than before, giving rise to a number of fine guitarists during the Be-Bop Era (and thereafter), like Jimmy Raney (with Stan Getz), Tal Farlow (with Red Norvo), Billy Bauer (with Woody Herman and Lennie Tristano), Arv Garrison (with Charles Parker), and studio guitarist Johnny Smith (with Stan Getz). Perhaps the most inspiring improviser of that group of guitarists is Jimmy Raney, who developed a flowing, graceful improvising style that always contained interesting note choices (sometimes deriving from *polychords,* the stacking of two unrelated chords simultaneously). Raney was also responsible for inspiring Stan Getz to one of his finest performances as a sideman on the album, "Jimmy Raney Plays," for which Raney was the composer. Ironically, Getz appears on the album under an assumed name, Sven Coolson, because he was under contract to another recording company. Getz' playing style was typical of the "cool school" (a restrained manner of playing) popular at that time.

The great master of jazz guitar, Wes Montgomery, was a self-taught player with a bittersweet career. Wes played with the Lionel Hampton Orchestra in the forties, and though already a very accomplished player and ripe for stardom, he returned to his home, Indianapolis, to live a more conventional and stable family life. It took him away from national exposure before he could rise to early fame, but the people in the Indianapolis area, especially the jazz musicians, were intensely aware of his mastery. Wes and his two brothers, Monk (bass) and Buddy (piano), teamed up with

Pookie Johnson (tenor) and Sonny Johnson (drums) to form a quintet that was legendary, performing for many years at the Turf Bar. It ranked among the finest jazz groups ever assembled. Individually, every player was an excellent soloist, and as an ensemble, their repertoire (mostly originals) was enormous, yet full of complexities in the arrangements, which were all played from memory. It was a perfect example of a group of self-taught players whose music nonetheless was expertly crafted and stylistically abreast (or ahead of) the times.

Wes Montgomery's improvising style was revelatory, especially in terms of building a solo to a point of climax, which he accomplished by playing the guitar in different ways (in themselves innovative). The first part of his solo, perhaps the first chorus or two, would be played as most players do, that is, in a single melodic line. Then in the middle of the solo, Wes would begin playing in *octaves* (two notes that are eight scale steps apart, bearing the same letter name but in different registers), which he could do at about the same speed as other guitarists would play single lines. Incidentally, most guitarists today will, at times, play in octaves in the manner invented by Montgomery. Then, in the next stage of his solo, Wes enlarged the octaves into tightly-compressed chords that moved in a melodic fashion, which harmonized his melodies. Finally, the compacted chords would open up into very full, widely spaced chords. By combining the various textures (single line, octaves, tight chords, and open chords), in their particular order, his solo would grow in intensity throughout its length, and the solo acquired an acute sense of order. Montgomery's sense for form also extended itself into the weaving of his melodies, each melodic fragment getting repeated, developed, and played in variations.

Suddenly, around 1959, Wes was rediscovered by the rest of the world, almost overnight, resulting in many semi-pop albums, in which Wes played tunes like "Goin' Out Of My Head" in octaves and little else. For those who knew him well musically, it was frustrating that he finally gained deserved recognition and economic reward for his genius, but at the expense of much of his musical greatness. Wes Montgomery died just a few years after his rediscovery.

Because Montgomery brought the guitar to perfection in the existing jazz style, it is natural that, after his death, the next great guitarists, with the exception of George Benson, played in a jazz-rock style that contrasted sharply with earlier guitarists. The new giants of guitar included Larry Coryell, John McLaughlin (with Miles Davis and Mahavishnu), and John Abercrombie (with Billie Cobham). Their manner of playing involves the use of string stretching (when it is applied to sustained tones, the pitch "yaws") and a profusion of electronic gadgetry, like phase shifters, reverberation, echo-plex, fuzz-tone, and cry-baby pedals, much of which originated in the rock style.

PIANO

Jazz piano has a very interesting history. Early jazz was heavily-dominated by pianists, and some of the jazz vehicles, like ragtime and boogie-woogie, were expressly developed for and by pianists. Many of the early bandleaders and arrangers were pianists. This trend continued through the thirties, when other instruments like saxophone and trumpet were on the rise, ascending to dominance in the forties and remaining dominant over piano during the fifties and sixties. But in the seventies the pianists are again dominant, led by players like McCoy Tyner, Herbie Hancock, Chick Corea, Keith Jarrett, and Joe Zawinul, all of whom are bandleaders, composers, and arrangers for major groups.

Ferdinand "Jelly Roll" Morton was one of the first well-known jazz pianists. Morton played as a solo pianist sometimes, and at other times in a trio (adding drums and clarinet); he also led the famous Red Hot Peppers Orchestra. Morton exhibited fine control of the keyboard, one aspect of that control enabling him to slow the tempo momentarily in his right hand, while maintaining an even pulse in the left hand, a feat demonstrated by Frederic Chopin in classical music. Morton claimed to have invented jazz. This is doubtful, but it is certainly true that his playing, his compositions and arrangements (which were extremely clever), and his leadership were valuable contributions to the development of early jazz.

James P. Johnson is sometimes referred to as the father of jazz piano for a variety of reasons. His recording of "Carolina Shout" was made in 1921, making it one of the earliest jazz recordings. His long career took him through several changes of style. For example, his early style was loosely based on ragtime, which he learned from listening to piano rolls and watching the motion of the piano keys.[6] By the late thirties, Johnson had adopted both the swing and the boogie-woogie styles. Boogie-woogie was based on the chord progression to the twelve-measure blues form. It was described as being "eight to the bar" because the left hand (carrying the pulse and the background) usually played eight notes in every measure. Boogie-woogie took the nation by storm. It was an exhilarating pulse for dancing because of the push of the double-time feeling, and it was an achievable feat of coordination for amateur or "parlor" pianists. Jimmy

Yancy, Meade Lux Lewis, and Albert Ammons also significantly popularized the boogie-woogie piano style.

Johnson's personal style, within any of the general stylistic changes he passed through, was always more modern than that played or other pianists within the same style. One

---

[6]Many piano rolls were made by pianist-composer of rags Scott Joplin. Joplin's music is known to many people today as a result of its exposure in the successful motion picture "The Sting." Also, composer-author Gunther Schuller's ragtime chamber orchestra, organized at the New England Conservatory in 1973, has featured many Joplin rags in numerous television appearances.

of his early recordings bore the symbolic title, "You've Got To Be Modernistic." Johnson was equipped with excellent piano technique, and his improvisations were filled with unexpected, clever, and modern elements, such as rich, extended chordal sounds and sudden but temporary changes of key in the middle of phrases.

Fats Waller was another influential pianist of the twenties and thirties. His humorous, rollicking style was captured not only on a number of recordings but also in printed piano arrangements that featured his many original tunes. Waller was extremely popular, particularly as a singer of clever songs, insuring that his gift would be noticed.[7]

Earl "Fatha" Hines was also active in the twenties, backing up famous singers on record, playing with luminaries like Louis Armstrong, and writing successful songs. Hines' career, like Johnson's, was long, still active in the seventies. Hines is credited with influencing a number of later pianists, like Stan Kenton and Nat "King" Cole. (Many people today are unaware of the fact that Cole, in addition to singing, was a major jazz pianist, winning jazz polls in the early forties.) Hines also led some star-studded orchestras, one of which featured the then young Dizzy Gillespie and Charles Parker, later to become leaders of the be-bop style.

Duke Ellington was also well known as a composer and bandleader of the first magnitude but it is seldom realized by jazz buffs that he was also a major pianist throughout his more than fifty years as an active player. He was already a well-known pianist in the twenties, and in the sixties he cut an album called "Money Jungle" with Charles Mingus (bass) and Max Roach (drums) that attested to his continuing ability to remain an authoritative performer in a perpetually blossoming state.

Perhaps the greatest jazz pianist of all time, both in terms of ability and influence, was the remarkable Art

---

[7]Two songs exemplifying the Waller wit are "Sam, You Made the Pants Too Long" and "Your Feet's Too Big." At the end of "Feet's Too Big" Fats indignantly asserts, "Your pedal extremities are obnoxious!"

Tatum, who recorded profusely for more than two decades (early thirties to middle fifties), turning out dazzling performances on hundreds of standard tunes. To describe his technique as "awesome" is somehow too mild a description. Even great classical pianists like Vladimir Horowitz praised and appreciated Tatum's absolute mastery of the keyboard. His harmonies were at least a couple of decades ahead of the times, and his pulse-feeling was flawless. If Tatum had a weakness, it was his lack of original, creative melody in his improvisations. For all that phenomenal technique, he seldom played an improvised melody of any degree of potency or lasting value. Nevertheless, great pianists like Oscar Peterson, Bud Powell, Clare Fischer, Hampton Hawes, and many others were inspired by the Tatum example. Tatum's best recordings are those in which he plays alone, as he liked to squeeze extra chords into the progression or invent breaks in an unplanned, spontaneous manner, which would have been curtailed by other instruments.

Teddy Wilson, chiefly through his work with Benny Goodman's trio and quartet, was highly regarded by jazz audiences and widely imitated by pianists of the thirties and early forties.

In the Be-Bop Era of the forties, the major pianists were Oscar Peterson and Bud Powell (both of whom had roots in Tatum) and Thelonious Monk. Peterson's style could be described as neo-Tatum. Powell, less emphatically influenced by Tatum, developed an original sort of left-hand style and improvised searing melodies that were very similar to the kind played by alto saxophonist Charles Parker. Up to the time of Parker, most instrumentalists had been influenced only by players who played the same instrument, but the Parker era ended that.

Thelonious Monk was (and still is) a jazz musician who plays and composes as an individual, seemingly unconcerned with the opinions of others about his highly unorthodox style. His touch (the way in which his fingers depress the keys) often sounds blatantly hammered out, as one might play "Chopsticks." His melodies are angular, rhythmically disjunct, full of notes that surprise the ear; and his chord notes frequently are so clustered together as to simulate a new version of "Kitten on the Keys." Nevertheless, he is a creative genius with a deep understanding of developing melodies in the manner of variations. The beautiful jazz ballad "Round Midnight," now a standard part of the repertoire of most jazz performers, was composed by Monk. Other Monk tunes that are widely played are "Straight, No Chaser," "Monk's Mood," "Epistrophy," "Bye-Ya," and "Ruby, My Dear." Monk is a musician without precedent, and few pianists have successfully adopted his style, though musicians of all instruments have been influenced by Monk's output.

Some of the well-known pianists of the fifties are Horace Silver (originally with Stan Getz, still leading his own group in the seventies), Errol Garner, Wynton Kelly (with Miles Davis), and Red Garland (also with Miles Davis). Garner and Garland form the first two links in a chain that revolutionized the modern-day pianists' left-hand chording style as well as influencing some aspects of the right hand.

In the late fifties and early sixties, the jazz world was blessed with the arrival of many superb pianists, including the major pianists as of this writing: McCoy Tyner (with John Coltrane), Bill Evans (originally with Miles Davis), Herbie Hancock (originally with Miles Davis, also), Keith Jarrett (originally with Charles Lloyd), and Chick Corea (with Miles Davis). Their careers are far from over, so that we needn't place them historically or pinpoint their styles and their contributions at this time.

It is worth mentioning here that many of the modern pianists are availing themselves of electric pianos, electronic gadgetry, and even electronic synthesizers. The addition of such instruments has added greatly to the repertoire of tone colors available.

The discussion of the rhythm section has not included all the names worth mentioning, nor has it included performers who play less-common instruments of the rhythm section, like Gary Burton (vibraphones) or Jimmy Smith (organ). But their importance to the jazz scene is not so much their accompmental capacities, as members of a rhythm section, but as soloists of exceptional ability.

FUNCTIONS OF THE RHYTHM SECTION

It was mentioned earlier that it would be absurd to call the Oscar Peterson Trio or the Bill Evans Trio a rhythm section, though the trios are made up of piano, bass, and drums, because they function as a complete group, not as a rhythm section waiting for the arrival of the horn players. But when those instruments are embellished by horns, then at least part of this function is to accompany and inspire the horn soloists. Individually, each member of the rhythm section is responsible for something that should be provided consistently. The drummer is responsible for time-keeping figures that will vary only slightly through the performance. The bassist provides a bass line and support the pulse, along with the drummer, by playing mostly steady quarter notes (one note per beat). The pianist or guitarist will supply the chord progression, supported by the bass line. The members of the rhythm section are individually and collectively responsible for responding to the rhythms and melodies of the soloist, which means that the drummer will play additional rhythms that are not part of the time-keeping figures, the bassist will occasionally alter his steady quarter-note approach, and the pianist or guitarist will improvise the rhythms with which they attack the chords, all in response to the soloist's needs for support. Responding does not necessarily mean to echo or imitate what the soloist has just played. It can also mean to fill open space left by the soloist between phrases or while he pauses to breathe or while he contemplates the next phrase. In other cases, the so-called response is actually an inspiring suggestion made to the soloist by the rhythm section or an individual in the section.

Collectively, it is very important that the rhythm section maintain a steady, unified pulse, retain good balance, keep place in the chord progression, guard the form of the tune, feel improvised introductions and endings (very common) together, raise intensity levels where needed, and anticipate opportunities to play rhythmic figures together in their improvised accompaniment.

The function of the pianist and that of the guitarist are, for all practical purposes, identical. Therefore, it is common to see rhythm sections which use either piano or guitar, but not both instruments, as they will collide as two drummers or bassists would, unless their functions, by prior agreement, are sufficiently different that they do not collide. Count Basie (pianist) solved the problem in his band by having his guitarist (Freddy Green) strum in steady quarter-note valued chords, while Basie used a very sparse left hand and played light, semi-melodic figures in the right hand. Miles Davis' group solved the problem in the album "In ' Silent Way" (Columbia CS-9875), which uses two electric pianos, and organ, and a guitar in the rhythm section, by approaching their improvised accompaniment not so much by chording in the conventional ways but by playing colorful sounds in different registers on instruments of different timbre (tone quality).

SUGGESTED LISTENING

Listen to an album by the Bill Evans Trio and/or the Oscar Peterson Trio to consider the functional differences (and similarities) between a piano trio and the more accompanimental function of rhythm sections you've heard on recordings of larger groups.

Many drummers, bassists, guitarists, and pianists were

mentioned in this chapter. The list below is intended to help the reader to locate recordings in the Smithsonian Collection that include samples of their playing. In a few cases, specific albums are recommended. Whenever a particular record is recommended, rather than a track from the Smithsonian Collection, consider the album significant enough to acquire for general listening as well as for hearing a particular player in the rhythm section.

Instrument	*Name*	*Recording Data*
drums	Baby Dodds	SC, side 1, track 6; side 2, tracks 6 and 7
drums	Gene Krupa	SC, side 4, track 3; side 5, track 4
drums	Sonny Greer	SC, side 6, tracks 4-8; side 7, tracks 1-3
drums	Kenny Clarke	SC, side 9, tracks 1 & 2; side 10, track 1
drums	Max Roach	SC, side 7, tracks 7-9; side 8, tracks 1-3; side 10, track 3; side 11, track 1
drums	Elvin Jones	SC, side 12, track 4; lp "A Love Supreme"[8]
drums	Art Blakey	SC, side 9, tracks 5 and 7
drums	Tony Williams	lp "Nefertiti," w/Miles Davis, Columbia CS 9594
drums	Billy Cobham	lp "Crosswind," Cobham, Atlantic SD 7300
bass	Jimmy Blanton	SC, side 6, tracks 7 & 8; side 7, tracks 1-3
bass	Oscar Pettiford	SC, side 4, track 5; side 7, track 5
bass	Milt Hinton	SC, side 5, track 6
bass	Slam Stewart	SC, side 7, track 4

[8]Impulse A-77. This lp has already been suggested in Chapter 1.

Instrument	Name	Recording Data
bass	Curly Russell	SC, side 7, tracks 6 & 7; side 8, tracks 3 & 5; side 9, tracks 2 & 7
bass	Percy Heath	SC, side 10, tracks 1 & 4
bass	Charles Mingus	SC, side 10, track 5
bass	Paul Chambers	SC, side 10, track 2; side 11, track 3
bass	Ray Brown	On most Peterson Trio lps (suggested above)
bass	Scott LaFaro	Could be on Evans Trio lp (suggested above)
bass	Charlie Haden	SC, side 12, tracks 1-3
bass	Ron Carter	lp "Nefertiti" (previously cited)
bass	Jimmy Garrison	SC, side 12, track 4; also on lp "A Love Supreme" (previously cited)
bass	Stanley Clarke	lp "Light As a Feather," Chick Corea, Polydor PD 5525
bass	Joco Pastorius	lp "Joco Pastorius," Epic PE 33949
banjo	Johny St. Cyr	SC, side 1, tracks 7 & 8; side 2, tracks 1, 5, 6, 7, 8
guitar	Eddie Lang	SC, side 3, tracks 4 & 5
guitar	Charlie Christian	SC, side 5, track 6; side 6, tracks 2 & 3
guitar	Wes Montgomery	lp, Milestone 47003
guitar	John McLaughlin	lp "Birds of Fire," Mahavishnu Orch., Columbia, KC 31996
guitar	John Abercrombie	lp "Crosswind" (previously cited)
piano	Jelly Roll Morton	SC, side 1, tracks 2, 7, & 8; side 2, track 1
piano	James P. Johnson	SC, side 2, track 4

piano	Earl Hines	SC, side 2, track 9; side 3, track 1
piano	Fats Waller	SC, side 4, track 1
piano	Meade Lux Lewis	SC, side 4, track 2
piano	Duke Ellington	SC, side 6, tracks 4-8; side 7, tracks 1-3
piano	Teddy Wilson	SC, side 3, track 3; side 4, track 3
piano	Art Tatum	SC, side 5, tracks 1 & 2
piano	Errol Garner	SC, side 8, track 4
piano	Bud Powell	SC, side 8, track 5
piano	Thelonious Monk	SC, side 9, tracks 4-8; side 10, track 1
piano	Oscar Peterson	on trio lp previously suggested
piano	Bill Evans	on trio lp previously suggested; also SC, side 11, track 3
piano	McCoy Tyner	SC, side 12, track 4; and on "A Love Supreme" (lp)
piano	Herbie Hancock	On "Nefertiti," previously cited
piano	Keith Jarrett	lp
piano	Chick Corea	lp "Light As a Feather" (previously cited)

4

THE IMPROVISED SOLO

Jazz music has always had a mystique about it. Perhaps that is true of music in general, but there is a special wonderment about jazz. What is this unique and alluring feature? We can probably rule out, although each makes its contribution in a general way, factors such as instrumentation, melody, harmony, rhythm, ensemble precision, dynamics (soft to loud), tempo, arrangement, and even time-feeling, because all of the foregoing are common to all musical styles. Is it because jazz was, in its infancy, associated with glamour, sex, liquor, and crime? That is unlikely, considering that the people who heard Jelly Roll Morton playing in a New Orleans bawdy house would now be seventy-five to a hundred years old, and no one could argue the fact that our national mores and morals have changed considerably since then. Furthermore, when jazz musicians play today, their thoughts, depending on the individual, will range from the physical to the divine, and in many instances they are too busy thinking of pure music to consider anything else. Much jazz is still performed in bars, of course, bars frequented by prostitutes, but most musicians accept those conditions to have a place to play, without feeling at one with the environment. Jazz today is performed in many other places as well, such as public schools, churches, city auditoriums, universities, municipal parks, television studios, motion picture studios, and the most successful in attendance and receptivity, the concert stages abroad.

Is the mystique of jazz related to the material and/or tunes performed? Are the tunes of jazz, often standard popular tunes, any more alluring than a Cole Porter tune, a Stevie Wonder tune, or any other kind of tune? Perhaps some of the jazz tunes are more energetic or cerebral, but not sufficiently so, and the listener will only hear the melody and/or words of the tune a short time at the beginning and end of the selection.

The awe-inspiring secret of the lure of jazz is improvisation. As it captured the imagination of the aristocracy in seventeenth and eighteenth century drawingrooms, where great composers such as Bach, Mozart, and Beethoven improvised from themes given them by members of the audience, improvisation is what captures the imagination of the person who listens to jazz. Jazz is the only music founded on the expressive craft of improvisation.

Spontaneous creation (improvisation) also charms audiences of improvisational theatre, improvisational comedy (such as The Committee or Jonathan Winters), improvisational poetry (ranging from traditional poetry to that of Muhammed Ali or Nipsy Russell), organ improvisation in church services, and even the light-hearted singing of improvised limericks by children at a party. But the pace of improvisation in jazz is more intense and more consistently applied. The excitement is in knowing that no one, on stage or in the audience, knows exactly what melodies will be woven by the soloists or what the accompaniment will do until the performance takes place. That is the mystique of jazz.

The listener can hear the improviser think, dream,

grapple with the instrument, the tempo, and the progression, be inspired by something happening in the rhythm section, become more intense, or falter occasionally. The improviser's spontaneous thoughts and feelings become transparent to his audience, who know they are witnessing active creation.

During a brewing improvised solo, those who know how to listen, understand, and appreciate the music not only catch the exciting scent of the brew, but can also look into the kettle and see what is there, able to identify some of the ingredients used in the loosely followed recipe. In this chapter the reader is urged to begin reaching for that level of understanding of the improvised solo.

A CLOSER LOOK AT THE VEHICLE

In Chapter 2 the vehicle was described as being a tune, standard or original, having the basic elements of melody, chord progression, rhythms, and sometimes words. The chord progression was mentioned as being the most important element to the improviser, though the present generation of jazz musicians have begun to investigate the potential of melody, rhythm, and words, as they might affect an improviser.

No mention was made, however, of how the specific nature of the chord progression affects the improvised solo. The progression could have a fast harmonic rhythm (as in "Giant Steps") or an inert one (as in "Mr. Clean"). The chords might be simple in structure (few notes, fundamental sound) or very complex (more notes, more dissonant sound). A fast or slow tempo will affect the improviser's approach to the progression, too. The mood of the tune and its progression are also considered by the improviser. The *sequence* of the chords in the progression is still another factor, ranging from common, traditional chord sequences to uncommon, unpredictable sequences. Bearing in mind that each of the foregoing characteristics of chord progressions affect the improviser's approach to playing his solos, then consider that he might encounter any of the following combinations of those characteristics:

	Tempo	*Harmonic rhythm*	*Sequence*	*Chord structures*
1.	fast	fast	common	simple
2.	fast	fast	common	complex
3.	fast	fast	uncommon	simple
4.	fast	fast	uncommon	complex
5.	fast	slow	common	simple
6.	fast	slow	common	complex
7.	fast	slow	uncommon	simple
8.	fast	slow	uncommon	complex
9.	slow	fast	common	simple
10.	slow	fast	common	complex
11.	slow	fast	uncommon	simple
12.	slow	fast	uncommon	complex
13.	slow	slow	common	simple
14.	slow	slow	common	complex
15.	slow	slow	uncommon	simple
16.	slow	slow	uncommon	complex

The mood of the tune would have to be added to any of the sixteen combinations, as would the style associated with the most popular recorded versions of the tune. Using the numbers given to the various combinations above, "Giant Steps" is a combination number 3, "Mr. Clean" is a 13, "Nefertiti" is a 16 (though we need a medium category for tempo and harmonic rhythm), "Maiden Voyage" is a 15, and "Pursuance" (Coltrane) is a 5. Although there are sixteen combinations, some of them are not likely to be utilized very often. A 4 would border on being too difficult, and a 13 would be dull, for example.

Certain other combinations will prove to be commonly used, because they describe certain families of tunes that are commonly played. Tunes having progressions like 7 or 15 (7 and 15 differ only in tempo) have component characteristics which collectively nearly define the *Modal* tune. Modal tunes have very slow (if not inert) harmonic rhythms, usually have an uncommon sequence of chords, and nearly always contain only simple chord structures. *Contemporary* tunes, when they are not modal, could be loosely defined as an 8 or a 16 (again, an 8 and a 16 differ only in tempo), using slow-moving, uncommon progressions with complex-sounding chord structures. *Be-Bop* tunes are mostly a 1 or a 3. The *Blues* tune has psychological and traditional approaches that are at least as important as the chord progression, and *Free-Form* tunes leave the chart altogether, as in most cases the chord progression is not assigned. The *Standard* tune can be any tempo, the harmonic rhythm is usually medium fast, the chord sequences are generally traditional (common), and the chord structures are relatively simple.

In a sense, we have just defined the six basic kinds of tunes, or vehicles, that are the most common in jazz; modal, contemporary, blues, be-bop, free-form, and standard. And their definitions are largely extant among the sixteen combinations listed. There will be further clarification of those terms, however, as the chapter progresses. Let it suffice to say, at this point, that these six kinds of tunes dominate the repertoire of the jazz musician, and the traits associated with those six types have much to do with the improviser's approach to playing his solo.

THE BE-BOP TUNE

During the *Swing Era* (1930–1940), characterized by big bands (15–20 pieces) and jitterbug dancing, jazz was more popular than at anytime before or after that decade. The proof of its mass popularity could be statistically realized by tallying box office receipts, record sales, radio air time, and other numerical sums, but the more significant proof could be provided only if we were able to return in time to the late thirties and interview the typical housewife or man on the street, where we could discover that they knew of and heard bands such as Count Basie, Duke Ellington, Benny Goodman, Tommy Dorsey, Artie Shaw, and Jimmy Lunceford in much the same depth and familiarity as the masses knew of rock groups of the sixties, like the Beatles, Chicago, Mothers Of Invention, Jimi Hendrix, or Blood, Sweat, and Tears. The Swing Era bands were appearing in a continuous cavalcade at local movie theatres, upstaging the Hollywood films that showed before and after the band played its show. The theatre marquee not only advertised the bandleaders, with great bannerlike signs and pictures, but also their featured sidemen (improvising soloists), because the masses knew them, also. Count Basie without his featured sideman, Lester Young, would have been like Mothers Of Invention without Frank Zappa.

Then came World War II, when the draft took away and/or displaced the bands (often the entire band would enlist to remain together and play overseas for servicemen), and a recording ban took away the records for one year. The Swing Era was over.

The young musicians who remained stateside during the war were concocting a new kind of jazz called be-bop. The period from 1940 to 1946 was an incubation period for be-bop, in which the music evolved and developed in relative seclusion, because of the war. By the time the war was over, the servicemen returned, and records were again being pressed, be-bop had drastically changed the sound of jazz. Technically and artistically, the additions and changes brought about through the experimentation of the early forties caused jazz to become an *art music* (music that develops at its own pace, artistically, regardless of consumption rate by the masses), rather than the folk-popular music it had been since the beginning. The masses turned away from jazz at this point, shocked and dumbfounded at recordings like

Dizzy Gillespie's "Things To Come" or Charlie Parker's "Koko."

Parker, Gillespie, Bud Powell, Thelonious Monk, Kenny Clarke, and Max Roach were the main perpetrators of the be-bop style, experimenting relentlessly with adding notes to chords, adding chords, changing chords, adopting fast tempos, changing the sound of the rhythm section, taking longer improvised solos, and reducing familiar melodies to their lowest terms. As was mentioned in Chapter 2, be-bop tunes were frequently based on the chord progressions to existing standard tunes. Often, however, the progression was slightly (at least) revised by adding or substituting chords. Parker, for example, took the bridge section of "I Got Rhythm" (a progression selected for many "new" be-bop tunes), which has only four chords, and by chord addition and substitution increased the number of chords in the bridge to sixteen. The increased chord motion caused the progressions to sound more interesting, but it also caused the progression to become more difficult to improvise upon. A jam session that included many be-bop progressions automatically excluded the player who could only play by ear or who was only familiar with standard chord changes.

Only the very strong survived the cutting sessions of be-bop days. But even the survivors adopted a playing manner that today is regarded as a stage of growth or a means to an end (rather than the end in itself). The increased pace of the harmony forced improvisers to spend most of their time spelling (with notes) the rapidly-passing chords, a practice known by jazz musicians today as *change-running*. From this we may learn that fast progressions, fast tempos, uncommon chord sequences, and complex chord structures all contribute to the necessity for change-running and inhibit melodic invention.

Jazz musicians still play be-bop tunes frequently, but chiefly as an exercise or discipline in change-running. This is not to say that change-running is without other virtues than, say, as a discipline to a growing musician. Such practice promotes harmonic clarity, rhythmic drive, and long, smooth musical lines. But it is true that pure improvised melody will be a secondary consideration. The fast tempo and progression encourage a steady stream of notes (as in change-running), whereas melodic (or lyrical) playing is more conversational in pace, using diversified rhythms, and having deliberate phrase endings. After all, be-bop progressions often move so quickly that, if you pause too long between phrases, several chords may pass unrealized.

If we listen carefully to Coltrane's "Giant Steps," for example, we notice that the swiftness of the progression causes his solo to be made up of long, steady, streams of notes (change-running) that could, in most places, be subdivided into four-note groups that lead into one another without interruption. Nearly every note of his long solo is an eighth-note value, rhythmically. There are two eighth notes to every beat, or eight eighth notes in every measure having four beats. As "Giant Steps" has a progression that changes chords every two beats, on the average, then there would be time to play four eighth notes to each chord, which explains the four-note subsidivions of his solo.

When subdivisions of this sort occur frequently and the notes within each group are arranged in a similar manner with successive chords, they are called *patterns*. To explain further, if the scale notes implied by each chord were given a successive number (see Figure 1), starting at the bottom or letter name of the chord as *1* and numbering upward through the scale with 2, 3, 4, 5, etc., changing the *1* to agree with each passing chord, and then apply this system to the notes actually played by Coltrane in "Giant Steps," it would be learned that he is re-using a few patterns many times. The four-note pattern, 1-2-3-5, for example, is used about thirty-five times in that solo, though often on a different or successive chord than where it first occurs (see Figure 2).

A pattern like 1-2-3-5 is very flexible. If the given chord is a C major chord, the notes corresponding to the numbers are C, D, E, G (1, 2, 3, and 5) (see Figure 3). If the chord is on

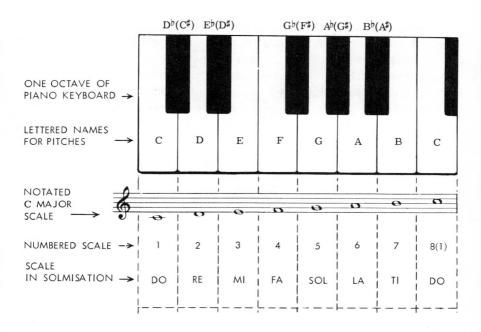

ONE OCTAVE OF PIANO KEYBOARD →

LETTERED NAMES FOR PITCHES →

NOTATED C MAJOR SCALE →

NUMBERED SCALE →

SCALE IN SOLMISATION →

CHORD SYMBOLS: (GIVEN)

LETTERED PITCH NAMES: B C♯-D♯-F♯ · D-E-F♯-A   G-A-B-D   B♭-C-D-F

NUMBERED PITCHES: 1 - 2 - 3 - 5   1 - 2 - 3 - 5   1 — 2 -3-5   1 — 2 - 3 - 5

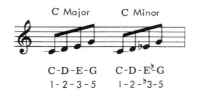

C, but is C minor, then the notes become C, D, E-flat, and G. Of course either the major or minor form can also be used, if needed, on chords built on notes other than C, simply by moving (transposing) the four numbers of the pattern to another note, making *1* synonymous with the new chord letter name and numbering up from there. Patterns are also flexible in that they can be played backward, often to equal or better effect, as in 5-3-2-1 (in such cases, *1* is still the letter name of the chord). Another variation of the pattern is to begin the 1-2-3-5 pattern on the fifth note of the chord-scale, so that the pattern is actually 5-6-7-9 or 5-6-7-2 (depending upon whether the numbers continue to ascend in the next register or restart after 7, since 8 will have the same letter name as 1). Coltrane used all these variations on the 1-2-3-5 pattern in "Giant Steps" and more, so that if they were also tallied as being related to, but not the same as, the 1-2-3-5 pattern, the total would far exceed the thirty-five occurances mentioned earlier.

Coltrane handled patterns exceptionally well, but the practice of using simple patterns and their variations is common to nearly all jazz players. It is no accident, either, as pattern-playing and/or change-running are logical approaches to the fast-moving progression of the be-bop tune, where there is little time to explore or be subtle with any single chord in the progression, much less develop pretty melodies. Virtually all players, as did Coltrane, practice patterns and their variations in daily practice as part of the preparation for the performance. The improviser doesn't decide in advance that he will use a certain pattern in a specific place in his solo, or that he will use the pattern at all, but practicing the patterns will help his playing, nonetheless.

Change-running and pattern-playing are essentially nonessential, being less original, more mechanistic, and less spontaneous than the more mystical model we hold in our minds for improvised music. In fact, much of such material is likely to enter the content of the improvised solo specifically at times when the player "hears" (images or conceives) nothing of interest. On the plus side, however, patterns train and quicken the mind and fingers of the improviser, improve his scope of hearing, introduce him to new aspects of harmony, enable him to better understand his favorite artists, give him springboards to creativity, and give him more time to be creative in other phrases (by providing material that can be played without thinking). And for the audience, patterns sometimes provide very intriguing sounds, and at other times, thanks to familiarity, the patterns may help us to understand many segments of the solo. At still other times, change-running patterns can help the listener to hear the chord progression, as it helped the player during his development.

It was mentioned earlier that the improvised solo is based on the chord progression. That is not to say that the progression itself supplies melodies, but rather that the chord tones (and the scales that fit the chords) provide the pitch choices, from which the improviser selects the pitches he wishes to use in his improvised melodies. A diminishing number of improvisers learn to find the chord and scale tones through the musical ear alone, without ever studying chord structures, scales, or progressions. If he has a *great* ear, the lack of such knowledge may never get in his way. But if he has only a *good* ear (or less), the challenge of finding the chord progression by ear is, to say the least, risky.

Most present-day improvisers learn the progressions by studying them in written form; then in performance, their intellect tells them what pitches are available and their ear joins with the intellect to help decide which of the available pitches will be chosen for the improvised melody. Such decisions are generally made during the solo (rather than before the solo is begun), perhaps a second or less before the phrase is played, a new decision being necessary for each chord of the progression. The studious player will practice interpreting all types of chords and the various scales which fit those chords (often a chord may have several scales that will fit it), in all keys and at various tempos. He does this, not so much to practice the creation itself as to prepare for the creation. However, much of what he practices will find its way into the creation, because of habit and from associating the practice phrase with the chord. The faster the tempo, the more likely it is that he will play what he practices, though perhaps in a slightly modified form.

THE MODAL TUNE

In 1959 the Miles Davis Sextet recorded an extremely significant lp, *Kinda Blue* (Columbia CS 8163). Its uniqueness lay in the fact that all the selections are *modal tunes*, which are nonexistent in jazz before that date. Several of the tracks became jazz standards, including "So What," "Freddie The Freeloader," and "All Blue." They were called *modal* because the tunes seemed to be updated versions of a large body of ancient (600–800 A.D.), modal melodies of the Roman Catholic Church, collectively referred to as the *Gregorian Chant*. The ancient chant melodies were based on *modes* (or scales), seldom changing modes within a given chant, and sung without harmonic or rhythmic accompaniment. The Davis group played tunes that were based on some of the same ancient modes, seldom changing modes within the tune, but adding a harmonic and rhythmic accompaniment. The *dorian* mode was by far the most widely accepted of the ancient modes that were revived by Davis's lp.

Within a few years after *Kinda Blue*, modality became a prominent part of jazz. The chord progression to a modal tune was described earlier as having a very slow (if not inert) harmonic rhythm, as uncommon sequence of chords, and simply-structured chords. Actually, modal tunes have a sort of nonprogression, in that the very few changes in chord provide sections of sharp tonal contrast that function more like the *B* sections of AABA tunes, rather than representing one chord (of many) in the smoothly connected chord sequence of a standard or be-bop tune. The long duration of each chord (at least 4-8 measures) contributes to the feeling that the modal tune is divided (by each chord) into relatively long, contrasting sections. The sections are long enough to obscure chord sequence, as the listener has probably forgotten the sound of the first chord by the time the third chord has arrived. So the modal tune's progression is not, in most cases, a common sequence of chords, nor is its harmonic rhythm fast enough to sound like smoothly connected chords in motion.[1]

Another important distinction of the modal tune's "progression" is that the name "chord" is also a misnomer. Because each chord has a long duration, the sound of the chord needs very little reinforcing after the first couple of measures. The listener still remembers the first announcement or attack of the chord, he has not been distracted by a change of chord, and the bass line continues to anchor the sound of the chord by building bass lines that reinforce fundamental notes of the chord. This is an extremely important aspect of modal playing, one that will be discussed again later in the chapter. For now, the point to be understood is that because the chord needs little reinforcing in the form of simple chord voicings (arrangement of the tones in the chord), the pianist, guitarist, the horn soloists, and even the bassist to some degree can treat each chord as though it were a *scale* (or mode) or a whole *key* area, greatly expanding on the older concept of simply producing a single, basic voicing for a chord, and then immediately preparing (in the mind) to play the next chord in the sequence. So to speak of a modal tune in terms of its chord changes only gives us a clue as to what is really going on. Contemplate the absurdity of applying change-running or short pattern-playing (i.e., the 1-2-3-5 pattern) to modal tunes. Both could be accomplished in the first measure of the "chord's" long duration. Then what?

[1]For a classical illustration, listen to the second suite of Ravel's "Daphnis et Chloe." Note the long durations of each chord and/or scale, and the dramatic bursts, into a new and contrasting chord/scale now and then.

How do we satisfy the voracious appetite of those durations to consume our patterns, chord spellings (change-running), scales, and ideas? Or contemplate the monotony of hearing the pianist or guitarists play the same chord voicing for, say, sixteen measures. Obviously, the approaches described for the be-bop tune are of little use to the improviser confronted with a modal tune.

A modal tune can be approached with patterns, but they need to be longer than the four-note patterns used in "Giant Steps." Improvisers have devised many patterns that move sequentially through the whole scale and can move up or down in range at will, so that it can last indefinitely! It is also worth mentioning here that the long "chord" durations also give the improviser time to investigate all notes of the scale, even the more remote tones of the scale that had to be omitted in the fast-moving progression.

The most important difference in interpretation, however, is that the improviser is freer to create thoughtful, formful melodies than he is when wrestling with a tune having a fast harmonic rhythm. In modal tunes he can select his pitches with more care, and he can pace the unfolding of his melodies to a more conversational level. He can also organize (spontaneously) his melodies so that they weave a musical tale that can be more interesting and varied, but as understandable to the listener as the preconceived melody to the tune. The logical development of improvised melody in variations was largely absent in jazz for the first fifty years of its history. Early players either played by ear, letting one melodic phrase lead into the next, or they knew the progressions but were led about by them into change-running.

In 1957 Sonny Rollins recorded "Blue Seven" (SC, side 10, track 3), which was the first time that a jazz improviser took on the challenge of *thematic* improvisation, that is, to improvise a long solo in which only two or three short melodic phrases (or *motifs*) are used, elucidating on each many times in variations. This recording was a very important contribution to the development of the jazz style in that it gave us a model for melodic form and development. It also held out hope for the estranged audience of jazz, because melodic unities would be the easiest aspect for an audience to comprehend. In 1964 John Coltrane recorded the album, "A Love Supreme," in which a single three-note motif (and its variations) is used to organize melodically the entire lp. Since that time, players like Wayne Shorter, Herbie Hancock, Chick Corea, and Freddie Hubbard have become intensely aware of utilizing fragments of the melody chorus in their improvised choruses. Many solos, even by the just-mentioned artists, do not yet contain such unities consistently, as melodic development is still new to jazz.

It is no wonder, then, that improvised melodies are so difficult to understand, as they are not usually (so far, anyway) derived from the given melody heard at the beginning and end of the selection. We can appreciate the sound, feeling, and rhythmic values of an improvised solo, but if we don't recognize or understand the improvised *melodies*, then a long solo may grate on our nerves and try our patience. We could, as listeners, give up trying to understand long, improvised solos, having decided that the solos are impaired by too much spontaneous creativity, making them too difficult to understand or remember. This would not be true, however.

The average improvised solo usually contains a high percentage of not so original and not so spontaneous material. Furthermore, there are times when the soloist only means for you to enjoy the sound, feeling, and rhythmic vitality of his solo. But the fact remains that we hope, as listeners, to understand, even anticipate, a reasonable percentage of the melodic events. Theorist-composer Richmond Browne once put it,

> The listener is constantly making predictions; actual infinitesimal predictions as to whether the next event will be a repetition of something, or something different. The player is constantly either confirming or denying these predictions in the listener's mind. ... the listener must come out right about 50% of the time—if he is too successful in predicting, he will

be bored; if he is too unsuccessful, he will give up and call the music "disorganized" . . . if the player never repeats anything, no matter how tremendous an imagination he has, the listener will decide that the game is not worth playing, that he is not going to be able to make *any* predictions right, and also stops listening.[2]

If we can raise our prediction percentage, maybe we can remain patient for some of those longer improvised solos.

Along with providing a vehicle for long pattern-playing and the development of melody, modal tunes also permit the improviser more time to use *intensifying* devices, such as a gradual increasing volume level, a slow rise in the range, a gradual thickening in terms of the number of notes used (rhythmic density), or an intensity rise effected by becoming more and more complex or dissonant, harmonically, throughout the length of the solo. The use of any or all of these intensifying devices will cause the solo to blossom, becoming more aggressively exciting as the solo develops. This also gives the solo a story-telling quality and pulls together all the miniscule phrases into a smoothly evolving whole.

It was mentioned earlier that the nature of the modal tune is such that the basic chord needs very little reinforcing, that the listener's memory and the anchoring bass line suffice to retain the sound of the chord, once a few measures have gone by. This realization by the performers has brought about a very common and interesting device, called *side-slipping,* in which the improvising soloist and/or the pianist or guitarist will slip into a key or chord that sharply contrasts with the given chord and then, after a brief time, slip back to the given harmony. All the while this is going on, the bass line generally stays in place, anchoring the peculiar motion and effect of the side-slip.[3]

---

[2]See pp. 15-16 of *Improvising Jazz,* Coker, Prentice-Hall, Englewood Cliffs, 1964.

[3]A close musical relative to the modal side-slip is *pedal point*, a traditional device in which the bass note is retained for a long duration, while chords move freely and chromatically against that unchanging bass note.

The use of the side-slip is not very predictable; that is, there is not a specific place in the solo or tune structure where side-slips happen, nor is there any way to know that a side-slip will be used at all, or that there will be few or many. To the unwary listener, it may sound as though a new part of the chord progression has been added or that the soloist is playing wrong notes. Only the anchoring bass line and the loosely implied structure of the side-slip give clues as to what is transpiring. The side-slip usually has at least some of the following characteristics:

1. it generally occurs on weak or unaccented beats or measures;
2. the foreign key gone to will be in total opposition to the given key;
3. the side-slip will usually be relatively short in duration;
4. it returns to the original key rather quickly; or
4a. it continues "slipping" indefinitely in the same direction; and
5. quite often the same melodic phrase or pattern will be used, first in the given key, then in a contrasting key, then once again in the given key.

Virtually all players today use the side-slip in modal tunes. The reader can test his ability to hear and recognize its use by listening again to Hubbard's "Mr. Clean"[4] and Coltrane's "Pursuance," both of which contain many side-slips.

THE BLUES TUNE

The blues are at least as old as jazz itself and represent a permanent part of every jazz player's repertoire. The chord progression to the blues is unique in terms of its twelve-measure length (traditionally, anyway), the chord sequence,

---

[4]In "Mr. Clean," the melody itself has a written side-slip, which occurs in the sixth and seventh measures of each melody chorus.

and the chord structures. It is a remarkable phenomenon in terms of its formal structure, being simultaneously more plastic and more resilient than virtually any piece of music ever written (or not written). We don't even know its sociological origin, much less its creator. The blues seem to have evolved almost simultaneously in cotton fields, in churches, in houses of prostitution, in the streets (the vendors), and in the music of the wandering guitarist-singer. W.C. Handy has frequently been named as its creator, having written the early blues, "St. Louis Blues." But he himself admits to having heard other blues tunes and/or the blues style prior to "St. Louis Blues."

We can be reasonably sure that the creator was a black man (or woman). Blacks have always exhibited unquestioned superiority in composing, playing, and singing the blues, and according to some historians the *blue notes* (certain altered pitches of the key) used so prevalently in jazz derive from the black man's attempt to shed much of his African music background in order to acquire the foreign (Euro-American) musical system presented to him by missionaries, resulting in a Euro-Afro-American scale, called the *blues scale*. The blues scale contains all three of the blue notes (lowered 3, 5, and 7). The scale, numerically spelled, is 1, ♭3, 4, ♭5, 5, ♭7, 8(1). In lettered pitches, from C, it is spelled C, E♭, F, G♭(or F#), G, B♭, C (see Figure 4). There are a couple of other versions of the blues scale, each using all three blue tones, but adding to or subtracting from the above example. In practice their differences are nearly indistinguishable.

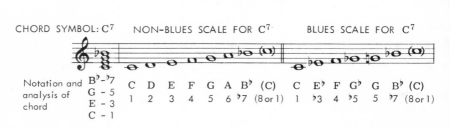

CHORD SYMBOL: C⁷   NON–BLUES SCALE FOR C⁷·   BLUES SCALE FOR C⁷

Notation and	B♭-♭7	C	D	E	F	G	A	B♭	(C)	C	E♭	F	G♭	G	B♭	(C)
analysis of	G - 5	1	2	3	4	5	6	♭7	(8 or 1)	1	♭3	4	♭5	5	♭7	(8 or 1)
chord	E - 3														
	C - 1														

Everything has been done to the blues in one version or another. There are blues that are different in length than the traditional twelve measures, blues that are not in four beats to the measure, blues that have more, fewer, or different chord changes, and blues of all stylistic varieties. Yet none of these alterations seem to improve upon the traditional version of the blues. In fact, the more the structure is changed, the less it sounds like a blues.

In other words, the blues carries with it many traditional values that are not encountered in be-bop or modal tunes and cannot be denied or ignored without risking an unsuccessful performance. The improviser prepares for a performance of the blues, not by simply studying the chord progression and/or gathering mechanistic patterns, but by carefully listening to well-known blues singers, such as Bessie Smith, Jimmy Rushing, Jimmy Witherspoon, Helen Humes, Joe Turner, and Joe Williams, paying attention to the general feeling, the phrasing, the time-feeling, and special effects. The improviser should also listen to recordings of great blues players, including Louis Armstrong, Sidney Bechet, Johnny Hodges, Lester Young, Charles Parker, Gene Ammons, Milt Jackson, Sonny Rollins, Charlie Mariano, and Miles Davis. Most of the foregoing list of soloists are noted for many contributions to jazz besides playing the blues, but each of them is a masterful blues performer.

Blues tunes, like modal tunes, have a sufficiently slow harmonic rhythm to allow the improviser to make use of intensity-building devices and formful melodies.

THE STANDARD TUNE

Standard tunes are not significantly different from be-bop tunes, in terms of the approach taken by the improviser. The chord progression is the primary mover, and it generally has a harmonic rhythm that is only slightly slower than the average be-bop tune (remember that standard tune progressions are often re-used as a foundation for be-bop tunes), and only a slightly more traditional approach to chord sequences and chord structures. Perhaps the chief difference is the wider range of tempos generally evidenced in standard tunes. Some Broadway show tunes that were originally performed in a typically medium fast tempo, felt in two beats per measure (on the first and third quarter-note beats), were adopted by jazz musicians and played in a very fast tempo, felt in four beats to the measure, emphasizing the second and fourth beats. Cole Porter tunes are often chosen for this sort of vehicle, as his long, gliding melodies sound good at tempos faster than they were originally performed. Like "Giant Steps," the melody moves slowly though the tempo is very fast. There are many standard tunes that make good vehicles for medium tempos, with more to choose from than would be found in be-bop literature, and far more slow ballads to choose from, as only a handful of be-bop ballads are in evidence, among them, Thelonious Monk's "Round Midnight."

Improvising a ballad is one of the great challenges in jazz. Some players can't slow to the pace of the tune, others falter harmonically by not selecting right and/or choice notes, and still others come up short in a melodic-lyrical way, failing to move the listener even as much as would the given melody to the tune. The great improvising masters of jazz history seemed to sense the importance of the ballad as a vehicle of distinction. After all, if you can't improvise a beautiful, creative melody in a ballad tempo, even with all the help and inspiration of rich, complex chords (much more prevalent in the ballad, where the ear has time to perceive such complexities), then something is missing—perhaps maturity and experience, or feeling, or love, or inspired creativity and craftsmanship. A great improviser can be gentle, pretty, and inspired in one situation, then become quick, steamy, and raucous for another, depending entirely upon the vehicle. The reader will probably discover, in his listening, that certain improvisers will often favor some of the vehicles we've discussed and lack experience, feeling, or ability for others. Coltrane and Mariano are good examples of improvisers who excelled on all vehicles, even some vehicles we haven't mentioned because they are too tangential stylistically or too rare to be included.

THE CONTEMPORARY TUNE

The contemporary tune was described earlier as being a vehicle with a slow harmonic rhythm (somewhere between the harmonic rhythm of the standard tune and that of the modal tune), uncommon chord sequences, and complex chord structures. It is one of the most difficult vehicles on which to improvise, requiring a deeper knowledge of harmony and greater versatility than in the vehicles discussed so far. Contemporary tunes sometimes combine two or more vehicular categories, each appearing in its own section within one chorus. For example, Herbie Hancock's "Dolphin Dance" uses typical contemporary devices (i.e., unusual chord sequences and structures) through most of the tune, with most of the chord durations being two or four beats long, then settles into a typical *modal* chord for four *measures* at the end of each chorus. Wayne Shorter's "Witch Hunt" begins with a sixteen-measure modal section (containing only two different chords, each lasting for four to eight measures), followed by eight measures of contemporary chords that change after each measure. Also, note that the tune's length is twenty-four measures, instead of the more common lengths of twelve (blues), sixteen, or thirty-two. Contemporary tunes often introduce new formal structures, seldom being an AABA form over thirty-two measures, as are so many of the standard tunes.

Contemporary tunes sometimes break away from the

four-beats-to-a-bar concept, also, or have sections that are played at half or twice the starting tempo. This writer recently encountered a contemporary tune by Ron Miller called "The Seventh Sign." One complete chorus of the tune was organized as follows: two ten-bar phrases, using contemporary harmonies and played as a bossa nova; a six-measure section that is modal (one chord), with a double-time feeling; a two-measure section in which the original tempo returns, six contemporary chords are played (at an average length of *one and one-half beats*!) in a complex rhythm that is collectively played by the whole rhythm section; an eight-measure section that is modal (an unusual mode, not dorian), but with a very free accompaniment, especially in the rhythmic sense, with a break (rhythm section suddenly stops) at the eighth measure; finally followed by a return to the first ten-measure phrase, making a total of forty-six measures for one complete chorus. "The Seventh Sign" should serve to illustrate why contemporary tunes are often the most difficult vehicles on which to improvise. Frequently the improviser, even the well-trained and experienced one, is asked to base his solo on materials (chords, scales, etc.) he's never seen or heard before (perhaps no one has). He can't prepare the next unpredictable task,[5] but he can learn as many as possible of the already-used devices he has heard, in the hope that the next unfamiliar experience will be less so.

THE FREE-FORM TUNE

In his search for a vehicle that would be nonrestrictive and allow complete creative freedom, the jazz musician invented *free-form*, or simply *free*, music. Around 1950 the

---

[5]For example, the recording musician sees the music for the first time at the studio (record date) and at the time of performance.

futuristic Lennie Tristano Sextet recorded a piece called "Intuition," the earliest recording of free-form music in jazz. All six players simply played whatever they wished. The result was subdued chaos, but it was a beginning, and remarkably ahead of its time, as free-form music was extremely rare until the late sixties, nearly twenty years after "Intuition," when the banner was again taken by up John Coltrane, Eric Dolphy, Miles Davis, Joe Henderson, Cecil Taylor, Chick Corea, Wayne Shorter, Freddie Hubbard, Archie Shepp, Pharoah Sanders, Roswell Rudd, and many others. Ornette Coleman's quartet was one of the few successful groups of the early and middle sixties to form their style around free music.

Free-form music can be approached in a number of ways, structurally speaking. The players could simply solo as individuals, without listening to or trying to be in coordination with each other. The effect, however, would be a jumble, like listening to four or five unrelated records simultaneously. Whereas such an effect has its place in music, it cannot be used too frequently or in long durations without being intolerably dull, monotonous, and lacking in drive. Consequently, most free tunes are based on at least one of the four cited elements of vehicles (tempo, harmonic rhythm, chord structure, or sequence) or some other trait, like mood, special scales, rhythms, or intensity-building devices. The surprising lesson learned is that the seemingly interdependent elements have great potential for organizing a disorganized free tune. Tempo is an important organizer, when adhered to by all members of the group. Adopting a specific number of beats in the measure will help, sometimes. The retaining by each instrument of some of its basic group functions will promote subtle organization (i.e., the pianist could concentrate more on providing chordal sounds, the bassist could provide bass lines and/or pulse some of the time, and so on). Or the group could agree that sections will last a certain number of minutes and seconds, or until a specific musical cue is played by someone, then try to find a contrasting feeling for the duration of the next section. Another subtle way to organize the piece is to agree ahead of time on the exact instrumentation that is to be used in each section, having some instruments withdrawn at times for variety in the overall sound of the group. Chaos results mostly from having too many people playing at one time, each trying to play a solo.

None of the foregoing organizational devices will unduly limit the improviser's creativity, but any or all of them will improve the performance. In many free-form pieces the players will adopt elements that are more restrictive, sacrificing some of their choices for a confident, clean and formful performance. Among such optional ingredients are chords, scales, tune structure, mood, certain *intervals* (distances between successive or simultaneous pitches), and given melodic fragments. Sometimes a free-form selection is helped by having total organization in some sections, such as a melody chorus or collectively played interlude sections between solos, but leaving other sections in which to be free and spontaneous.

The improviser prepares for the free-form performance in much the same way as for the approach to contemporary tunes, but a free tune or performance is even less predictable than a contemporary tune, so the search to acquire any new device is slightly intensified to include some *atonal* (without a key) patterns and even some *extramusical* devices (unorthodox sounds, often without a specific pitch, like squeaks, mechanical key noise, vocal yelps, electronic static, and countless other possibilities). As strange as these sounds are, they must be practiced as diligently as the more conventional music sounds, if they are to be used effectively. The devices should not inhibit the seriousness of the craft.

Some aspects of the improvised solo are not necessarily related to the vehicle and therefore have not been discussed before now. The remainder of this chapter will discuss them.

HABITS

Some of the melodic material in the improvised solo is derived from change-running, patternized disciplines—or, put more simply, habits. Some habits are of an aural nature, established both in practice and in performance, causing the player to consistently choose the same phrase against certain chords of the progression, sometimes even to choose the same sequence of phrases (by association). Needless to say, the level of predictability increases sharply at those times. Other habits are of a physical nature, such as the times when an improviser plays a phrase chiefly because the phrase, in addition to fitting the chord, is comfortable to the fingers, owing to its ease and familiarity. This practice can also lead the musician to repeat a whole sequence of phrases in the same order each time. Still another kind of habit is the mental one, in which the player is liable to think of the same phrase on the same chord each time, as he sees (or remembers) the chord symbol.

CLICHÉS

An artist who has recorded many, many solos isn't likely to have an inexhuastible supply of ideas that defy repetition altogether, and many of his musical ideas are an integral part of his personal style, relatively sustained, like his physical appearance, his diet, or his signature. Such ideas are sometimes referred to as his *clichés*, and all great players have had them. Their disciples usually acquire their masters' clichés before tackling other traits of their solos. An audience can likewise become familiar with a soloist's clichés.

QUOTES

In addition to change-running, patterns, and clichés, we can expect, in the average improvised solo, melodic fragments that derive from a different soloist within the same performance, from an influential player of the time, or from another tune altogether (sometimes referred to as a *quote*). Sometimes a quote from another tune is used because the subject matter of the lyrics are similar, sometimes because the melodies are similar, sometimes to be humorous, and other times simply because the quoted melody fits the chord progression of the tune being played. As mentioned earlier, the soloist will sometimes use fragments of the given melody (the melody usually heard at the beginning and end of a selection), either to establish melodic form or simply because he is hearing the original melody at that moment.

ORIGINALITY

What remains in the solo if we extracted all change-running, patterns, chichés, and quotes? Surprisingly less than you'd imagine, perhaps 0% to 20% in most solos. Now there can still be originality, in that the player may have created his own patterns for practice, and his weaving together of this, his own less-spontaneous material, may have shown creativity at work. Or there can be overriding factors, like emotional quality, rhythmic feeling, tone quality, clarity, energy, phrasing, even some sorts of cleverness.

After all the less spontaneous segments (habits, quotes, etc.) are extracted, the remainder is the creative heart of the solo. Not all of this more original and spontaneous portion of the solo is necessarily inspiring or enormously successful, but this is where we would look for the soloist's more original creations. To explain the source for this more creative content is like trying to explain the origin of life. We can talk about the conditions, environment, and elements, as we explained away patterns, clichés, and quotes, but the creation itself remains one of the unsolved mysteries. Even the statement made earlier to the effect that the composer's output is chiefly the product of what he has heard in prior listening to others does not sufficiently explain the source of some astoundingly spontaneous and creative melodies that have sparked an otherwise average improvised solo. It is interesting to note, also, that it is sometimes very difficult to estimate a young player's potential for such inspired invention until he has acquired the more mundane aspects of his soloing (patterns, clichés, and quotes), at which time he will either use such mundanities as a springboard to originality, or it will become obvious to the listener that the control and disciplines acquired through practicing patterns, clichés, and quotes are the extent of his creative ability. So the truly creative phrases are a rarity, even in the accomplished improviser's solos. Happily, though, it is nearly always so, that the more original phrases enjoyed by the improvising player are often the most enjoyable phrases to the audience as well. Indeed, a well-attuned audience can usually detect an improviser's best performances, as in the case of jazz festivals, where an audience that is well-prepared through prior listenings is able to appreciate a particularly inspired performance by an artist they may have heard many times before.

REPAIRING ERRORS

Jazz, being largely improvised, is a difficult style to perform and record in a flawless fashion. Only a few performers have been consistently perfect in their execution of improvised solos. Consider some of the ways in which an artist can commit an error. His fingers might momentarily be uncoordinated, causing an unintended, incorrect pitch. His ear might fail him in a more spontaneous moment of attempting to play a phrase by ear. He could misread a chord symbol in his haste, or his eyes (if he's reading the chords) can accidentally skip or repeat a line of music on the page. If he's not reading the chords, he could forget a chord of the sequence, or lose his place with respect to the form of the tune, as in arriving at the bridge (middle) section of the tune at the wrong time. If he's a brass player, his lip may fail him. Students of jazz who have transcribed improvised solos find that, in addition to wrong notes, they are likely to discover phrases which are uneven, rhythmically. It would be an understatement to say that the good jazz improviser has to be resourceful with respect to transforming errors into successful phrases. One common method is to quickly slide from a erroneous pitch into a correct one nearby. Or he might even repeat the error and its correction on some other note within the key, reinforcing the illusion of deliberation. If the error causes the player to experience several "false starts" on a phrase, perhaps because he's become finger-tied trying to execute it, the choppy rhythmic effect created by the false starts can give the solo an intensified and unique rhythmic feeling, if the player deliberately continues to repeat the accident. Another way to salvage a bad note is to sustain and/or repeat the note, using it as a springboard to what is commonly referred to as *playing outside*, which simply means deliberately playing in contrast to the given chords. Believe it or not, there are musical justifications for doing this, for example, the tension created by side-slipping. So, as a final ingredient to improvised melody, we must consider the accidents and their resourceful solutions. Nearly all improvising players are accident-prone, even the great ones (who partially make errors because they are especially spontaneous, courageous, and creative, taking more innovative chances). Some players consistently play perfect solos because some or all of the solo is a contrivance, worked up before the performance. I personally prefer to listen to players who are not that insecure, as I prefer creativity and spontaneity to perfection. Sometimes, though rarely, a player comes along who is both innovative and consistently flawless, as in the case of Charles Parker.

SUGGESTED LISTENING

Player/Group	Title/Album	Recording Data	Listening Objective
Coltrane	"Giant Steps"	Atlantic SD-1311	harm. rhy., patterns
Hubbard	"Mr. Clean"	CTI 6007	modal, side-slipping
Davis	"Nefertiti"	Col. CS 9594	contemporary
Hancock	"Maiden Voyage"		harm. rhy., modal
Coltrane	"A Love Supreme"	Impulse A-77	thematic, side-slipping
Gillespie	"Things to Come"	Rondellette A-11	contrast w/ swing era
Davis	"So What"	SC, side 11, track 3	modal
Rollins	"Blue 7"	SC, side 10, track 3	blues, thematic
Smith	"St. Louis Blues"	SC, side 1, track 4	blues
Smith	"Lost Your Head Blues"	SC, side 1, track 5	blues
Mingus	"Hora Decubitus"	SC, side 10, track 5	be-bop blues in minor
Parker	"Parker's Mood"	SC, side 8, track 3	blues

Player/Group	*Title/Album*	*Recording Data*	*Listening Objective*
Armstrong	"Potato Head Blues"	SC, side 2, track 7	blues
Armstrong	"S.O.L. Blues"	SC, side 2 track 6	blues
Armstrong	"West End Blues"	SC, side 2, track 9	blues
Bechet	"Blue Horizon"	SC, side 2, track 3	blues
Hancock	"Dolphin Dance"		contemporary
Shorter	"Witch Hunt"		contemp.–modal combined
Shorter	"Chaos"		free-form
Fischer	"Free Too Long"	Pacific PJ-52	free-form
Henderson	"Mind over Matter"	Milestone M 9034	free-form
Davis	"Shhh/Peaceful"	Col. CS 9875	free-form
Taylor	"Enter Evening"	SC, side 11, track 2	free-form
Coleman	"Free Jazz"	SC, side 12, track 3	free-form

5

THE
IMPROVISERS'
HALL
OF FAME

In 1959 Gunther Schuller delivered a lecture pertaining to jazz history on the campus of Sam Houston State University. In the question and answer session that followed, he was asked why his list of jazz greats was so short (about a half dozen or so) and if its brevity reflected the belief that jazz had not produced many extraordinary players. Schuller replied by pointing out that classical music took several hundred years to produce the number of great composers equal to his list of great jazz improvisers, which took only sixty years to amass. Schuller then reaffirmed his attitude as being, contrary to what was implied in the question, very positive.

There are so many impressive players, each making some sort of contribution to the idiom, that it is difficult to reduce the number to what would be reasonable for the scope of this book and for the capacity of the reader to absorb. Guidelines were followed as an aid to making objective choices. First of all, only well-known greats are included to assure access to their music. (There are great players who remain secluded, relatively unknown, and therefore seldom recorded.) The list also does not include supportive players, such as bandleaders, lead trumpet players, arrangers, or rhythm-section functionaries. Many of the impressive young players of the seventies have been omitted, awaiting further development and/or the test of time. Not every player on the list is a genius, though some probably are, but they are innovative enough to influence large numbers of improvisers. If our "Hall Of Fame" included only six artists, they would be Louis Armstrong, Lester Young, Charles Parker, Miles Davis, Coleman Hawkins, and John Coltrane. If the "Hall" could accommodate twelve, then the additional six players would be Sonny Rollins, Dizzy Gillespie, Thelonious Monk, Clifford Brown, Herbie Hancock, and Freddie Hubbard.

Although the list was made without regard to the instruments played, five of the twelve are saxophonists. Saxophone has been a popular instrument in jazz, but more importantly, it is an easy instrument to learn, easy to control, and it is capable of the kind of expression, phrasing, and tone quality heard in the human voice. After all, if the instrumentalist is relatively free of problems relating to the playing of the instrument, then his thoughts can more often be directed toward the content of the solo.

CRITERIA FOR APPRECIATION

There are three basic approaches to serious listening: *criticism,* by very carefully scrutinizing the performance, taking special notice of all weaknesses and errors, and determining whether or not there is something left to enjoy; *evaluation,* in which the listener places a relative value of each aspect of the performance and is interested in both the sum total of its worth and, on a sliding scale, the value of each of its parts or aspects; and *appreciation,* in which the listener takes special notice of the strengths of the performance, even in small details, and is less concerned with flaws, either ignoring or tolerating them. All three approaches are careful, perceptive, and objective, but there are mild differences of attitude, with respect to hearing positively and negatively, so that the approach taken should agree with level and function of the listening. A judge at a music festival needs the first approach (that function requiring a high level of training and experience) because the performing groups are generally strong and well-matched, and the performances are short and in rapid succession. He doesn't have time to write down everything he hears, but he has to mention the unusual qualities of each group, both to help him to remember each band amid many and to help him with his final decisions of comparison. The judge is more concerned with taking off points for imperfections than in adding points for good qualities, though he will also consider the other two approaches to listening from time to time.

The budding jazz musician needs the second approach (evaluation) in order to maintain efficiency in his listening. He needs to hear a lot of music. As some of the pieces need repeated listenings, he needs to be aware of exactly why he's listening to it (to absorb its strengths more efficiently). He can't afford the time to listen repeatedly to weaker performances.

The reader probably needs the third approach, appreciation. Both the judge and the budding jazz musician have already learned to enjoy the music and have dedicated their lives to it, whereas the reader may be less convinced by, and dedicated to, listening to jazz. Hence, the listening attitude needs to be positive, at least for a while, especially to work at raising the levels of appreciation and patient tolerance.

Here is a list of criteria for appreciating jazz improvisers:

> *Sound:* the tone quality, which can range from small to large, mellow to brilliant, or dull to lively. Nearly all jazz players can be identified by their sounds alone.

Technique: the speed, evenness, and clarity of execution (finger dexterity, etc.).

Time: the consistent accuracy and feeling of the pulse. All great players are perfect or near perfect in this respect.

Tonal materials: the selected (there are often choices) chords, scales, and emphasized melody notes (in improvisation). The listener probably won't know exactly what is being used, but he can notice a difference in the sound of the selected materials, especially in the case of pretty or effectively used melody notes.

Spirit/drive: the emotional feeling and the vitality and conviction of the rhythms and pulse.

Lyricism: melodiousness.

Repertoire: the selected vehicles, their general types (modal, blues, standard, etc.) and their specificity.

Versatility: the inclusion of many vehicle types and their corresponding approaches and feelings, or simply, the capacity to change without becoming less effective.

Innovation: the qualities of inventiveness, creativity, and originality.

These criteria will be used for the remainder of this chapter to help describe and appreciate the variegated qualities of the players in our "Improvisers' Hall Of Fame." To ensure a proper perspective of the historical development of jazz, the players will be covered in chronological order. Nicknames for the artists will be given in parentheses below their full names, to aid the reader in knowing when a player is being alluded to in a tune or album title, or in conversation and books. For example, if you didn't know that one of Armstrong's nicknames is "Pops," then you wouldn't know that Louis is the person to whom the Thad Jones–Mel Lewis album, "Suite To Pops," is dedicated. Or when you see "Bird Lives" written on a wall somewhere, you won't know that it refers to Charles Parker.

LOUIS ARMSTRONG (1900–1971)
(Dippermouth, Satchmo, Pops)

Louis Armstrong's position in the Improvisers' Hall Of Fame is unique. His career got under way almost simultaneously with the beginning of recorded jazz (the early twenties) and close to the beginning of jazz itself (around 1900). Unlike the other players of this chapter, his improvising style had to evolve largely from within, having few precedents to lead the way or provide inspiration. Buddy Bolden (1878–1931) preceded Louis; he was reputedly one of the very first jazz musicians and, according to Jelly Roll Morton, the most powerful trumpet player of early jazz. But Bolden went insane before jazz was being recorded and before the very young Armstrong (seven years old when insanity ended Bolden's career) could be influenced by his playing. Morton himself was practically a contemporary of Armstrong's and probably exerted little influence on his playing. Joe "King" Oliver, whose band was Armstrong's stepping stone to stardom, was a highly respected cornet (close relative of the trumpet) player during Louis' youth and influenced him considerably. But within a short while after Armstrong joined the Oliver band, Louis was the better player of the two. Oliver, Mutt Carey (another early trumpet–cornet player), and singer Bessie Smith probably influenced his approach to playing the blues, but by and large, Louis was on his own, with little jazz history on which to reflect.

Although each of the players in this chapter is an innovator in the jazz style, it is interesting to contemplate the possible effect on their careers of a similar lack of forerunners. If improvisers lean heavily, in the creative sense, on all the music they've ever heard, as pointed out in prior chapters of this book, then consider how much more varied was the listening of Freddie Hubbard, for example, compared to that of Armstrong. And also consider the difference in the volume of recorded jazz heard by these two players. The record makes it possible to re-hear any spontaneous creation endlessly, if desired, even to the point of transcription to musical notation, analysis, and total absorption.

Early jazz players (e.g., Joe Oliver and Freddie Keppard) were reluctant to have their improvisations recorded (or their arrangements, for that matter) during the first years of recording, as they recognized the opportunity for other players to re-hear and carefully copy anything they had on record and feared the ensuing competition for work and fame, once their secrets were known and assimilated. History shows that their concern was not without cause, as imitators have often crowded or displaced their stylistic idols by way of their race, business acumen, production talents, or simply their easy, local availability. Musically, though, imitators learn, rather than steal, from those to whom they listen (and they generally listen to many players on records, not one). Individuality is inescapable, so that no two players sound exactly alike, regardless of any effort made to that end. Furthermore, improvised music often needs re-hearing by the audience, to increase the level of their appreciation.

Armstrong was also the first great star of jazz. He was massively popular, a powerful player, an awesome entertainer, an irresistible singer, and a joyous spokesman for jazz. It would be difficult to estimate how popular jazz would have been without "Satch," but in many foreign countries he is the only known jazz figure.[1]

The blossoming of Armstrong's playing can be experienced on record. Listen to his playing on "Dippermouth Blues" (SC, side 1, track 6) with Joe Oliver's Creole Jazz Band in 1923, where Louis is more or less absorbed by the ensem-

---

[1] Armstrong drew 93,000 people for a concert in the Budapest (Hungary) Football Stadium in 1965.

ble, playing second cornet to Oliver. Or listen to "Cake Walking Babies" with the Red Onion Jazz Babies in 1924 (SC, side 2, track 2), where he is eclipsed by the soprano saxophone playing of the great Sidney Bechet. Then listen to the Hot Five and Hot Seven recordings of 1927 (SC, side 2, tracks 5-9), where Louis suddenly explodes into prominence. The listener no longer has to listen carefully to hear a little of Armstrong's playing. He is more audible, prominently displayed as a soloist, more confident and witty, and vastly more expressive. Armstrong's close affiliation with Earl "Fatha" Hines (piano) in the late twenties resulted in additional flowering for Louis, and he acquired considerable finesse during the thirties, leading and soloing with a big, semicommercial band. But the period 1924–1927 is still the most significant of his blossoming experiences.

Armstrong's stylistic development was complete in the early thirties, sophisticated and perfect in execution, and his style remained relatively constant to his death in 1971, forty years later. He lived and played through the years of Swing, Be-bop, Post Be-bop (1950–1960), and Modern Jazz without permitting those styles to effect much, if any, change in his personal style of the early thirties. Nearly all players have a tendency to change less after their initial blossoming-maturing period, but Louis changed far less than the other players of this chapter. Miles Davis, John Coltrane, and Sonny Rollins are players of perpetual change, for example.

When the "Criteria for Appreciation" are applied to the extraordinary improvisers of this chapter, it will be found that certain players are more distinguished, even partly identified, by certain of the criteria, while other criteria may not be of any real consequence to his greatness. His exaggerated strength in a few areas can cause the listener to be blissfully unaware of the relative absence of (not weakness in) other areas.

Armstrong's *sound*, for example, is strongly associated with his musical personality. It is big and full of vitality, and sustained notes are subject to being embellished by an intense vibrato (especially at the end of the note), a slide up to the note (at the beginning of the held note), or a slide down from the pitch at the end. His sound is volatile, urgent, and expressive. And his unique tone quality is easy to recognize among the tone qualities of other trumpet players, never having been duplicated by anyone. Listen to "S.O.L. Blues" (SC, side 2, track 6) or "12th Street Rag" (Harmony HS-11316) and experience the power of Armstrong's sound in the form of jabbing high, long notes. That sound, first noticeable in the 1927 recordings, was largely responsible for his blossoming at that time, projecting him permanently into notice.

Louis' *technique,* in terms of speed, might not impress the listener after hearing, say, Gillespie, Brown, or Hubbard, but his technique was abundantly sufficient to handle the style of his generation, and he was generally considered to be a virtuoso. He seldom faltered, his high range wouldn't be challenged for at least a decade, and he seldom "cracked" (lost control of) his notes, though he incorporated many wide, difficult leaps from one note to another in his solos. Louis' solo on "Struttin' with Some Barbeque" (SC, side 2, track 5) illustrates both his speed (i.e., the break he plays halfway through his solo) and his wide melodic leaps. Another aspect of his technique is his masterful control of the *squeeze,* an upward, evenly sliding pitch that sounds muffled or held in until it bursts into a loud, high note at the end. It is effected by pushing the valves of the trumpet halfway down while slowly tightening the lips. Examples of his use of the squeeze may be heard on "Shine" (Harmony HS-11316), "Sweethearts on Parade" (SC, side 3, track 2), and the best example on "I Gotta Right to Sing the Blues" (SC, side 3, track 3).

Armstrong's *time* was perfect in every respect. He played a pulse that was both accurate and emphatic, even in long breaks where he played alone. Louis often spoke of the importance of "swinging" rhythmically. His control of the pulse also extended into rhythmic and metric areas as well. For example, he could play the tempo in half-time (in 2) or double-time, he could change quickly, in the middle of a phrase, to widely diversified subdivisions of the beat (rhythmic levels, like eighth notes, triples, etc.), he could play the meter (time signature) of 3/4 against a 4/4 background, or even play a phrase that deliberately is out of time with the given pulse. Some of Armstrong's breaks sound as though he's testing his band's ability to count their way through the break and re-enter at the proper time. One of the best examples of Louis' penchant for rhythmic diversity is his playing of the first melody chorus of "12th Street Rag," in which he places the repetitious three-note motif of the given melody on virtually every conceivable place within the measure, in constantly changing rhythmic levels. Ironically, the melody of "12th Street Rag" is, in its written form, already an implication of a 3/8 meter against the 4/4 meter. The recording is doubtlessly more than a hint of Louis' humor.

The modern listener's first impression of Armstrong's use of *tonal materials* might be deceiving. Older music sometimes strikes us as simplistic in sound, and indeed Louis did approach many chords in a simple, almost buglelike manner. But careful examination of his note choices, especially when compared to other players of his generation, reveal that he used his total materials in highly imaginative ways. For example, in "Basin Street Blues" (Harmony HS-11316) Armstrong repetitively plays phrases which are based on one note of the given key of the tune. However, the tune has a number of chords, some of them being remote from the key, so that Louis' single, emphasized note is being re-used for each chord, creating a variety of harmonic effects. The simpler-sounding notes of a chord are usually the 1, 3, or 5 of a numbered scale fitting the chord. The more complex-sounding notes are the 7, 9 (or 2), 11 (or 4), and 13 (or 6). Louis' repeated note, then, functions as 3 of the first chord, 1 of the second, 5 of the third chord, 9 of the next, and 13 of the next! The effect is both economical and harmonically rewarding. Also, with respect to tonal materials, the vehicles used by Armstrong were not simplistic. The formal structures (i.e., AABA) and their overall lengths were sometimes more complicated than modern tunes, and the progressions often moved in a fast harmonic rhythm and through chords that are remote from the key or starting place. Yet Louis moved gracefully through the paces set by the vehicle. In his solo breaks, Louis sometimes changed chords to give the break harmonic motion, though no one else was playing at the time or forcing him to change chords. He also played very effectively over *stop-time* backgrounds (where the accompaniment is only playing short chords on important downbeats, leaving the rest of the measures blank, similar to the break) with relatively complex progressions, giving the soloist little time to absorb the sound of each chord. "Potato Head Blues" (SC, side 2, track 7) is a good example of Louis' ability to handle stop-time choruses without faltering, with respect to tonal materials.

For anyone who has heard any of the Armstrong recordings, especially since 1927, it is redundant to speak of his *spirit* or *drive,* as they are ever-present. His *lyricism* cannot be questioned, either. His singing style and his playing style are identical. To borrow a well-used phrase, he "sings" through the horn. Listen to the superb phrasing of the given melody in the last chorus of "Struttin' with Some Barbeque." At times Louis sounds as though he is sobbing or crying joyously with his explosive high notes.

Armstrong's *repertoire* and *versatility* are not as important to an appreciation of his playing as they might be with later players. While he used rags, marches, standard tunes, gospels, and blues, his material can mostly be relegated to standard or blues vehicles, since most vehicles used today had not yet been invented. He was versatile within those vehicles that did exist, but his style remains virtually unchanged throughout his career.

Innovation is almost synonymous with everything he played, as there were so few precedents for much of what he chose to express. He invented many of the clichés that were

adopted by all Dixieland groups, swing era players like Roy
Eldridge (trumpet), and even Dizzy Gillespie. After 1930,
Armstrong did little to advance innovative new jazz styles,
but his contributions until that time were unparalleled.

After describing each of the artists in this chapter and
discussing them in terms of the criteria for appreciation, a
particular solo will be chosen for closer analysis. The annotated, blow-by-blow analysis should aid the listener in becoming better acquainted with, and more appreciative of, one of
the best solos. It is suggested that the listener first hear the
whole selection, then read the analysis, then re-read the
analysis while re-hearing the solo portion of the selection.
(This last stage may need to be repeated a few times.) For
Louis Armstrong, the selected performance is "Shine," recorded shortly after his blossoming stage.

LOUIS ARMSTRONG on "Shine" *(Harmony HS 11316)*

vehicle type:	Standard
formal structure:	A(8)-B(8)-AB(8)-C(8)
arrangement:	4-measure introduction
	melody chorus
	vocal chorus (slower tempo)
	scat vocal chorus (return to fast tempo)
	soprano saxophone and drum breaks (short)
	2 improvised trumpet choruses
	long break (with drums), followed by chord

Analysis/Annotations

1. Note the change of chords at the end of his break (in the
   introduction), that leads into the first note of the melody
   chorus. He makes this change by himself, as the others in the
   group are not playing.

2. Listen to what he plays in the ninth measure of the melody chorus (the beginning of the B section). He has departed from the melody, momentarily, and plays a simple, but effective change-running idea on this somewhat remote chord of the progression. This same idea will recur two more times in the first improvised trumpet chorus; the first is at B again (ninth measure of that chorus), the second at the short B section in the AB portion (twenty-first measure) He also sings the same sequence of notes *backwards* in the scat vocal chorus at the short B section again, this time adding several successive variations to fit the next chords.

3. The melody used in his break of the fifteenth and sixteenth measures (end of B) of the melody chorus is not the melody to "Shine," but an improvised *quote* from the tune "Pretty Baby."

4. Observe, in the second half of the melody chorus, the jutting, breathless phrasing of the melody, so typical of the Armstrong style.

5. Notice how he delays the phrases of the vocal chorus, making up his own lyrics (words) much of the time.

6. The use of breaks by another member of the band, between the vocal and trumpet segments, is typical, permitting Louis enough time to pick up his horn.

7. His trumpet solo, a masterpiece of economy, is almost entirely based on two notes. There are other notes played, but the certain two notes are emphasized by sustaining and/or repeating them and by placing them at the top of the phrase's range. He begins the solo by playing only the note B-flat for the first eight measures, unpredictably attacking it thirteen times in the lower register, then squeezing up to a high B-flat, then adding two more attacks in the lower register.

8. He again squeezes up to the high B-flat (a much longer squeeze this time) in the break before his second chorus.

9. Now he begins repeating the high B-flat, much in the manner of the beginning of the solo (where he used the lower B-flat), but also introduces the second note to be emphasized, G, by using it repeatedly as a pickup note to the B-flat.

10. At this point (B section of the second chorus of the trumpet solo), he begins emphasizing G, re-using it against several

successive chords, retaining the G as the primary note of the familiar bugle-like break that follows.

11. After the break he squeezes from G to B-flat, reminding the listener of both emphasized notes, then concentrates heavily on the G for the remainder of the AB section.

12. Without warning, Louis suddenly begins to insistently alter the G (which was 3 of the key E-flat) to G-flat, giving a blue-note effect that alludes to Joe Oliver's frequent use of the blue note, except that Louis also continues to juxtapose the G against the G-flat, by rapid alternation.

13. In the long break (with drums) at the end of the selection, Armstrong returns, for the first time since the introduction, to the chord he changed to in the last four notes of the intro-duction. This time he uses that chord for the first eight mea-sures of the break with the drums. That particular chord has a G-flat in it, which permitted Louis to continue emphasizing that note.

14. Then the G-flat is dramatically changed to G after exactly eight measures of the break, then moves in semi-tones up to the high B-flat, on separate attacks, then uses the high B-flat as a pickup note to his final note, E-flat, which is the keynote of the tune but which Louis withholds from emphasis until the very last note, where it would be the most effective.

It would be misleading and inaccurate to imply that all the unifying factors mentioned in this sort of analysis were deliberately planned or thought about by the improviser, before or during the improvisation. Many such unities are instinctive and natural to the performer of great ability, training, and experience. Hence the listener, who is gener-ally less experienced, may need to have these unities pointed out to him until he begins to *instinctively hear* them.

Finally, a quotation from Louis Armstrong himself:

> When I blow, I think of times and things from outa the past that gives me an image . . . a town, a chick somewhere back down the line, an old man with no name you once seen in a place you don't remember. What you hear coming from a man's horn, that's what he is.

ARMSTRONG DISCOGRAPHY

At the Crescendo, MCA 4013 (2 records)

Best of Louis Armstrong, Audio Fidelity 6132

Essential Louis Armstrong, Vanguard 91/92 (2 records)

Golden Favorites, Decca 74137

Great Reunion with Duke Ellington, Roulette 52103

Hello Dolly!, Kapp 3364

Hello Louis, Metronome 510

Hot Fives And Seven, Decca 74230

I Love Jazz, Decca 74227

I've Got the World on a String, Verve 64035

I Will Wait For You, Brunswick 754136

King Louis, Decca 74245

Louis Armstrong, Audio Fidelity 6241

Louis Armstrong, Harmony HS 11316

Louis Armstrong and Earl Hines/1928, Smithsonian Associates
   (2 records)

Louis Armstrong with His Friends, Amsterdam 12009

Louis Armstrong with the Dukes of Dixieland, Audio Fidelity 5924

Louis in the '30s and '40s, RCA 2971

Louis Meets Oscar Peterson, Verve 68322

Louis Plays King Oliver, Audio Fidelity 5930

Louis "Satchmo" Armstrong, Archives Of Jazz And Folk Music
   258

Louis under the Stars, Verve 64012

Mame, Pick 3229

Rare Batch of Satch, RCA 2322

Rare Items, Decca 79225

Satchmo—Autobiography, Decca 78963, 74330, and 74331

What a Wonderful World, ABC S-650

(plus the ten selections by Armstrong in the Smithsonian Collection)

COLEMAN HAWKINS (1904–1969)
(Hawk, Bean)

The listener who is familiar with the playing styles of both Louis Armstrong and Coleman Hawkins will probably find it difficult to realize that their life spans nearly coincide. The young listener might have considered both to be "older players," but it is doubtful that he would have thought them to be contemporaries. When Louis was launching his career with Joe Oliver's band in 1923, Coleman Hawkins was starting his career with the Fletcher Henderson Orchestra. Both bands had roots in the New Orleans style of early jazz, but Henderson's band quickly developed a style that sounded more like a very early swing band, like those heard in the thirties.[2] In fact, Henderson wrote many of the arrangements that catapulted the Benny Goodman big band into national prominence in 1936.

Louis' stylistic development is relatively complete by the early thirties and remains virtually unchanged after that. "Hawk," on the other hand, could have stopped his stylistic development at about the same time as did Louis, as he was already an accomplished player by then, but he didn't stop. Instead, he continued to absorb new styles for the rest of his life, creating considerable change in his style from decade to decade. In the early twenties he sounded like a Dixieland or New Orleans-styled tenor saxophonist, as he did on "St. Louis Shuffle" with the Henderson band (RCA LPV-501). Several years later (1929), on "One Hour" with the Mound City Blues Blowers, Hawkins, in addition to acquiring maturity and individuality, sounded more like a swing era player of

---

[2]Strangely enough, Armstrong played with the Henderson Band in 1924–1925.

the thirties. In the mid-thirties, a legendary group of all-night sessions took place in Kansas City, focusing on a musical battle among the three major tenor saxophonists of that time, Hawkins, Ben Webster (from Duke Ellington's band), and Lester Young (from Count Basie's band). As a result, Hawkins absorbed aspects of their styles. For example, he began using the buzz-tone or growl-tone used so frequently by Webster, effected by humming and blowing simultaneously, as well as some of Webster's angularity (wide, unpredictable leaps). In "Hocus Pocus" (RCA LPV-501) there are very strong allusions to the Young style. The arrangement sounds like a Basie band's arrangement and is in the key of D-flat, a favored key of the Basie band when showcasing Lester Young, which perhaps that influenced Hawkins' concept for improvising on the tune. He played three of Young's more obvious clichés, reduced the number of notes from what usually occurred in a Hawkins solo to a sparseness that agrees more with the Young style, and treated some of the chords in ways that are more common to Young's solos. Webster's solo style was relatively close to Hawkins' style, so any borrowing of ideas between them would be less noticeable. Lester Young, however, was a controversial player who developed his own approach to sound, vibrato, chord interpretation, and density (relative number of notes used). Young was encouraged more than once to adopt the more-established styles of Hawkins and Webster, but no one ever suggested that Hawkins or Webster move closer to Young's style. Yet "Hawk" did just that on "Hocus Pocus," though he did not retain that closeness on successive recordings. At other times in his career, Hawkins played the blues close to the style of Paul Gonsalves (of the Ellington band) or Arnett Cobb (of the Lionell Hampton band). Around 1944 Hawkins recorded "Half Step Down, Please" (RCA, LPV-501) with a group of be-bop musicians. Again, he adapted to the situation by using be-bop ideas and materials in his solo. In the early sixties he recorded with an unlikely team mate, Sonny Rollins, in the album "Sonny Meets Hawk" (RCA 2712).

Hawkins was nearly sixty years old at the time and Rollins was only in his early thirties, yet Hawk was again making the effort to change to a more modern concept for improvising, as evidenced in "All the Things You Are."

All in all, Hawkins' career of changing styles contrasts sharply with Armstrong's consistent personal style. The changes that took place in Hawkins' approach were not so complete as to remove all former aspects of style. He retained much of his early style through the years, but even so he showed great flexibility in meeting each new challenge.

His sound was large, husky, and warm, heated further by a deep but fluctuating expressive vibrato that sometimes identifies him. Because of the similarity between his sound and that of Ben Webster, and because both were widely admired and imitated (by, for example, Chu Berry, Herschel Evans, Don Byas, and Paul Gonsalves), it is difficult to be absolutely certain at times but, generally speaking, Hawkins can be recognized largely by his sound. It was not an overwhelming sound, like that of Armstrong, but it was a very rich tone that had dynamic mobility; that is, he moved the volume and intensity levels up and down rather rapidly, even within a single melodic phrase. Although the Hawkins sound was the standard model for the saxophonists of the thirties, the Lester Young sound became the model for the next two decades, as heard in the playing of Stan Getz, Paul Quinichette, Brew Moore, Herbie Steward, Al Cohn, Zoot Sims, and Bill Perkins. (Curiously, all of the foregoing except Paul Quinichette are white musicians. As Quinichette was Young's replacement on the Basie band, he needed to reflect upon the giant who preceded him.)

Hawk's technique was, even in the early days, extremely swift and facile, flawless, smooth, and graceful. This is a point of distinction between Hawkins and Webster, in that the latter's technique was more spontaneous, less inhibited, and therefore a more difficult sort of technique to control, at least to the degree exhibited by Hawkins. It might take a well-trained jazz musician to detect that difference, however, as Webster's technique was also exceptional (listen to Webster on "Cottontail" with the Ellington band). Between his vibrant sound and extraordinarily smooth technique and phrasing, Hawkins' notes seemed to melt with warmth and become as a liquid, waves of volume, wavelets of vibrato.

His time-feeling was perfectly precise, though gentler than Armstrong's and not so bluntly adventurous. Armstrong's sparse hammering style lent itself to playing widely displaced accents or the layering of one time signature upon another (i.e., 3/4 across 4/4), Hawkins' rhythmic style, on the other hand, was a more continuous stream of notes, very smoothly played and more subtle in its rhythmic effect, though his pulse-feeling in a blues or a fast tempo was generally more emphatic. He frequently used the double-time effect in ballads, but he seldom used half-time feelings in tunes that were played in a fast tempo.

One of the most obvious characteristics of Hawkins' improvisations was his handling of tonal materials. Heavily laden with change-running ideas, his solo lines investigated each and every chord of the progression, emphasizing the bass line with sudden descents to bass tones in the middle of phrases, and including virtually all resolving tones of chords. (Certain notes of chords lead naturally into certain notes of the next chords in a progression, called *resolving tones* or *tones of resolution* which, when used properly, can create the aural illusion of chord motion, even when all notes of the chord are not present in the solo line). Hawkins was so intensely aware of his tonal materials that often in "How Deep Is the Ocean" (RCA LPV-501), the accompaniment is unnecessary, as his emphasis of chord notes, bass line, and resolving tones are sufficient accompaniment in themselves.

Whereas spirit and drive were never lacking, lyricism was perhaps a mild weakness in Hawkins' playing. He phrased given melodies beautifully and frequently employed formful variations in successive improvised phrases, but he seldom created memorable, singable melodies. He did, however, amply compensate for this lack with other characteristics.

Repertoire and versatility, on the other hand, were typical of his playing. He played standards, blues, Dixieland tunes, ballads, be-bop tunes, and popular songs, and was heading toward contemporary vehicles at the time of his passing. He was extremely versatile with respect to style (traditional, swing, be-bop, etc.), as well as vehicle type.

A mild lack of lyricism and the tendency to *follow* trends are not characteristics which support a case for innovation, but his sound, vibrato, perfect technical control, phrasing, use of tonal materials, and stylistic flexibility created a highly admired model for at least two generations of tenor saxophonists.

COLEMAN HAWKINS on "How Deep Is the Ocean" *(RCA, LPV-501)*

vehicle type:	Standard (ballad)
formal structure:	A(8)-B(8)-A(8)-BA(8)
arrangement:	4-minute piano solo introduction
	loosely placed melody chorus by tenor saxophone, with rhythm section accompaniment
	improvised chorus by tenor saxophone, with soft horns and rhythm section accompaniment
	improvised cadenza by tenor, followed by chord

Analysis/Annotations

Coleman Hawkins was an extraordinary improviser of ballads. He also played the blues and fast tempos commendably, but great ballad players are rare, and it was his classic solo on "Body And Soul" (1939) that established his reputation for inspired mastery of the ballad. Three of his ballad solos were under consideration: "Body And Soul," "Say It Isn't So," and "How Deep Is the Ocean." The last was chosen, somewhat arbitrarily, because it contains a slightly greater number of Hawkinesque elements.

1. Note the progression, which has both slow and fast harmonic rhythms and contains chord sequences that descend in semitones (chromatic). It also uses an interesting device in the first four measures of the A sections; the chord is the same for all four of the measures, but the bass line descends chromatically, producing a change of scale without actually changing the chord. Listen carefully and you can hear this device taking place in Hawkins' solo at many points in both choruses. Often it will sound as though he is playing the descending bass notes, but adding many other notes in between each of the longer, emphasized bass notes. The progression to the entire selection would have been apparent, in sound, even if there had been no accompaniment other than Hawkins's self-accompanying phrases.

2. Listen to the vibrato of his opening phrase and at the end of the selection. He is sometimes identified by that vibrato, though it is deeper and more pronounced than on perhaps any of his recordings.

3. Listen to the manner in which Hawkins phrases the melody in the first A section (his first entrance). Because he is loosely rendering the melody and because he is implying the progression between the melody phrases, it would be helpful to listen to a recording of the tune by a group or player playing the given melody in its purest, simplest form, so that the listener will know which of Hawkins' notes are from the given melody and which are not.

4. Hawkins decorated the melody so heavily in the next two sections (B and A) that the given melody is mostly implied, and in the last eight measures of his first chorus (BA) he has virtually abandoned the given melody altogether. Jazz players in general were beginning to adopt such practices to allow

more time for creative improvisation. This became unnecessary with the invention of the long-playing (33-1/3 RPM) record.

5. The harmonic device mentioned in #1, in which the first four measures of the A sections have only one chord but in which a descending bass line causes changes in scale, produces an interesting scale in the second measure of those four measure sections, called the *whole-tone scale*. The name derives from the fact that only whole steps (two semi-tones equal a whole step) are used in constructing the scale, causing the scale to have a distinctive sound. Listen to what Hawkins played the second measure of his second chorus, where he used the whole-tone scale, not in a way that sounds like a scale, but like descending chord patterns. In the eighteenth measure of the second chorus (which is also the second measure of an A section), he plays a nearly identical pattern. As mentioned in Chapter 4, improvisers often hear (in their mind's ear) the same pattern against the same chord repeatedly.

6. Another example of the association between pattern and chord was supplied by "Hawk" in the twenty-first measure of the first chorus, the fifth measure of the second chorus, and the twenty-first measure of the second chorus. Each of the three locations are identical, harmonically, all being the fifth measure of an A section, and he treated each of these places with the same improvised melody (which has an arresting double-time feeling).

7. Notice the density of notes in the sixth measure of the second chorus, where he played six notes per beat, deftly. The density level is noticeably greater throughout the second chorus, which, along with the entrance of the horn background, served to raise the intensity level.

8. The third time he played the double-time idea mentioned in #6, he repeated the idea sequentially through the chords of the twenty-second measure (of the second chorus), leading into the highly intricate, embellished sequences of the twenty-third and twenty-fourth measures. "Hawk" finally got finger-tied on the last one of those embellishments (going into the twenty-fifth measure), unfortunately, but it is doubtful that anyone else could have executed it as well, much less

conceived such a phrase. Hawkins' sequential phrases and fancy embellishments can be found on nearly all of his recorded solos.

9. Like Louis, "Hawk" sometimes speared relatively high notes suddenly after subdued phrases, as a preacher might employ the device to regain the attention of his audience. This trait is evident in many other solos, including "Body and Soul." In "How Deep Is the Ocean," he used the device twice, on nearly identical phrases, in the twenty-sixth measure of both choruses.

10. The tempo stops on the thirty-first measure of the second chorus, where Hawkins played his virtuosic cadenza, again creating the sound of chord motion without relying upon accompaniment.

HAWKINS DISCOGRAPHY

Bean Bags, Atlantic 1316

Blues Groove, Prestige S-7753

Body and Soul, RCA LPV-501

Classic Tenors, Atco FD 10146 and Contact CM-3

Coleman Hawkins, Archive Folkways 252

Coleman Hawkins and His Orchestra, 1940, Alamac QSR 2417

Coleman Hawkins and the Trumpet Kings, Emarcy 66011

Desifinado, Impulse 28

Essential Coleman Hawkins, Verve 68568

Good Ole Broadway, Prestige MV23

Hawk Eyes!, Prestige 7857

Hawk Flies, Milestone 47015 (2 records)

Hawk Relaxes, Prestige MV15

Meditation, Mainstream 6037

Night Hawk, Prestige 7671

No Strings, Prestige MV25

Live at the Village Gate, Verve 8509

On the Bean, Continental 16006

Pioneers, Prestige 7648

Sirius, Pablo 2310707

Sonny Meets Hawk, RCA 2712

Today and Now, Impulse 34

Wrapped Tight, Impulse 87

(plus two selections by Hawkins in the Smithsonian Collection)

LESTER YOUNG (1909–1959)
(Prez)

Lester Young might be described as a second generation jazz musician. His rise to prominence began in the mid-thirties, more than a decade after Armstrong and Hawkins were launching their careers. As might be expected, his style contrasted with the early jazz style of the twenties. Young once put it, "I play *swing* tenor." He is best known for his long association with the Count Basie Orchestra, where he was featured more than any other player to come through the ranks of the Basie organization. He was sometimes given several solos, separated by ensemble passages and/or another soloist, within a single selection. Lester played with other groups and sometimes led his own small groups, but he is chiefly remembered for the Basie years, specifically 1936–1940. Some critics have argued that those were his best playing years, and that, contrary to Armstrong's maintaining his peak stage of the late twenties, or Hawkins' continuous development, Lester actually declined in stature (in spite of continued admiration).

It is true, perhaps, that the recordings of the fifties for the Norman Granz (producer) labels (Norgran, Verve, Clef, etc.) show a lessening of vitality, more flaws, poorer command of the instrument, and other signals of decline, even imminent physical collapse. Those recordings are nonetheless cherished by jazz musicians. For one thing, Young had, by then, gone through a mild change of style, partly because of the influence of the be-bop style, but also because of his own development and maturation as an artist. He lightened his sound, played more ballads, searched for newer, fresher notes, developed a feeling of lagging behind the pulse, explored the limits of relaxed improvisation, and was more occupied with sounding pretty. Unlike Hawkins, that was his only change of style, and it was not an especially dramatic change. Nevertheless, "Prez" (for "President") was a stronger influence on be-bop and post be-bop ("cool" jazz of the early fifties) musicians than was "Hawk." The Jimmy Giuffre composition "Four Brothers," recorded by the Woody Herman Orchestra in 1947, was dedicated to the Lester Young style and featured three of his best-known protegés, Stan Getz, Zoot Sims, and Herbie Steward, on tenor saxophones, plus Serge Chaloff, a Parker-influenced baritone saxophonist. Bill Holman wrote a composition of a similar nature for the Herman band of 1954, called "Prez Conference." When it was recorded, the title was changed to "Mulligan Tawny," but the tenor soloists Bill Perkins, Dick Hafer, and Jerry Coker were all under the spell of the "Prez" style. His closest imitator was Brew Moore, a relatively unknown tenorist of the fifties who recorded with Gerry Mulligan.

Lester Young's sound was his most distinctive trait, though not his only musical innovation. Our ears first hear the nature or quality of a sound, then perhaps go on to hearing the many interrelationships of notes, in terms of phrases, high and low pitches, rhythms, and so on. Perhaps it is because of the immediacy of quality perception, not needing a whole phrase in which to incubate. Or maybe it's because, in the atavistic sense, we are in the instinctive habit of first considering whether the sound hitting our ears is friend or foe. That is, is it the sound of a familiar voice, a siren, something breaking, a growl, or a machine's hum? For whatever reason, we do judge or identify first the quality of the sound, and Lester's sound was unique. It was not especially large at any time, and sometimes it was extremely light. The sound was broad and flat, with little air behind it, as might be simulated by someone trying to expend as little energy as possible, striving to achieve the totally relaxed state, including the lip muscles, while playing. It was not a lively sound, and the vibrato was slight and inconsistent. Some described it as "dead tone." Yet "Prez" used that sound in very expressive ways (with the phrasing devices), ranging from funky to poignant, and it was his sound that imitators sought to duplicate first.

Young's technique was adequate and he used it in interesting ways, but he didn't develop or use it to the degree evidenced in Hawkins' playing. But then the Young style was a sparser approach, using fewer notes and considering each more thoughtfully, an approach that is similar to that of Miles Davis on trumpet.

In his early years of recording, "Prez" played with a time-feeling that was right on the beat, punctuated, and aggressive. By the fifties, he had changed to a relaxed, almost lagging approach to the pulse.

Young's handling of tonal materials was thoughtful and creative. He favored certain notes against certain types of chords. Players who understood this were better able to identify him on records or to play more like him. Naturally, he used all notes everyone else did from time to time, but he emphasized certain ones. For example, his familiar device of repeating a single note for a rather long while usually took place on 1, 6, or the lowered 7 of the chord or key in which he was playing. When he swooped or slid up to a long note, another of his traits, the object note (the long one) was usually 3, 5, or 7 (as the lowered form of those numbers are the three blue notes, the slide up to 3, 5, and 7 simulated a blue tone effect). It was mentioned earlier in the book that, when using numbers to represent the scale notes, 2, 4, and 6 can also be called 9, 11, and 13, respectively. The numbers used in building chords will generally be the odd numbers only, as in the 1-3-5-7 spelling of a seventh chord. This keeps one note of silence between each chord tone, as the 2, 4, and 6 are not used, but when they are renumbered to 9, 11, and 13, appearing in the next highest register, they are now odd numbers and can be added to the top of the chord, with silent members 8, 10, and 12 in between (8, 10, and 12 would be redundant, as they are the same notes as 1, 3, and 5 in the lower register). If, then, we were to stack all the chord notes (represented here in numbers), the sequence, from bottom to top, would be:

$$1-3-5-7-9-11-13$$

Inasmuch as the scale has only seven different lettered or numbered notes, it is apparent that all seven possibilities appear in this sequence. This sort of addition to the chord, called *extension,* makes the chord richer in sound.

Furthermore, some of the chord tones can be raised or lowered by a semi-tone, to create even more possibilities. "Prez" favored certain of these possibilities, such as the raised 5, the 9, and 13. One of the most common note sequences of his later years was a 9 resolving down a semi-tone to the lowered 9. The addition of 9, 11, and 13 to a chord was especially common in the be-bop era, remaining in use to the present. Young also had an affinity for the *pentatonic scale,* a five-note scale that would be numerically represented by 1–2–3–5–6. His use of the pentatonic scale was especially prominent in the recordings made with Basie. Today the scale is an integral part of jazz, especially in modal tunes. "Prez" also used an early version of side-slipping, by moving successive phrases down in semi-tones against an unchanging harmonic background. In selecting particular keys for tunes, Lester showed a strong preference for A-flat and D-flat, a unique trait in itself. Quotes were fairly common in his playing. For example, in the melody chorus of "Mean To Me," he played a four-measure quote from "Easy Street," as the tunes have identical chord progressions in their A sections.

As was mentioned earlier, Young's spirit and drive waned in his later years, but his lyricism increased over the years. To be more specific, he was perhaps the most melodious improviser in jazz history, especially in the fifties, in spite of the possible decline in other areas of his playing. His music has a gentle quality to it. Furthermore, as an exceptionally thoughtful player, he needed to be relaxed and needed time to consider each phrase, even each note, that might delay an artistic decision about the next phrase to be played, possibly affecting both time-feeling and drive. The ebb and flow of our creative powers have to be reckoned with. When we are held up by the ebb, we can stop playing, play something relatively uncreative (i.e., a pattern, a scale, a change-running idea), or wait another mini-second or two for a good idea to present itself in time to be played.

Young's repertoire was almost entirely made up of blues and standards. He was a master of the ballad, a setting which could accommodate his gift for creating melodies. He was not especially versatile, with respect to vehicle types or overall style change. He was an innovator of the first magnitude (in sound, note choices, phrasing, etc.), and his influence upon the jazz style was, and is, considerable.

LESTER YOUNG on "Lester Leaps In" *(SC, side 6, track 1)*

vehicle type:	Standard (It is an original melody, but borrows its chord progress from the standard "I Got Rhythm.")
formal structure:	AABA (each section is 8 measures long)
arrangement:	See the table on page 100.

Each of the "A sections" of the THIRD CHORUS is made up of 6 measures of "stop-time" (defined in glossary),

		A	A	B	A
INTRODUCTION	number of measures: 4 (piano solo with bass and drums accompaniment)				
FIRST CHORUS	section:	A	A	B	A
	no. meas.:	8	8	8	8
	action breakdown:	ensemble melody--------		rhythm section	ens. mel.
SECOND CHORUS	section:	A	A	B	A
	no. meas.:	8	8	8	8
	breakdown:	tenor solo------			
THIRD CHORUS	section:	A	A	B	A
	no. meas.:	6 + 2	6 + 2	8	6 + 2
	breakdown:	stop-time-time	stop-time--time-----	time---- time	stop-time-- time
		tenor solo-----			
FOURTH CHORUS	section:	A	A	B	A
	no. meas.:	4 + 4	4 + 4	4 + 4	4 + 4
	breakdown:	piano-- tenor--piano--	tenor--piano--	tenor--piano--	tenor--piano-- tenor--
FIFTH CHORUS	section:	A	A	B	A
	no. meas.:	3 + 5	3 + 5	8	3 + 5
	breakdown:	ens.-- tenor----ens.--	tenor----ens.--	piano------	ens. -- tenor ---
SIXTH CHORUS	section:	A	A	B	A
	no. meas.:	3 + 5	3 + 5	8	3 + 5
	breakdown:	ens. -- bass--- ens. --	bass--- ens. --	bass ------	ens. ------

followed by 2 measures of "time" (time-keeping, in which there are no interruptions of the played pulse).

The following analysis will cover only those portions of the selection that featured Lester Young. To avoid confusion, all specific locations within the selection will be identified by using the table, with its numerical and verbal designations. If reference is made to, say, the second chorus (of the selection), it will not be confused with the second chorus of his solo.

1. Notice the partial quote of the "Lester Leaps In" melody, played by Young at the beginning of the SECOND CHORUS.

2. Immediately after the partial quote, he played a descending sequence of notes that is the pentatonic scale mentioned earlier.

3. In the next A section, he played a repetitious phrase based on the lowered 7, then another repeating sequence that alternated between 5 and the lowered 5, resulting in a segment that sounds "blue."

4. Toward the end of that second A section he again played the pentatonic scale in a descending direction, as cited in #2 of the analysis.

5. The bridge melody of "I Got Rhythm" is implied by "Prez" for about the first six measures of the B section (still in the SECOND CHORUS).

6. In the last two measures of that B section, he descends on a series of notes that might sound, to the listener, as though he had played another pentatonic scale; however, it was actually a phrase that incorporated two of his favored notes, the raised 5 and the 9 of the chord.

7. Young liked to use repetitious figures, sometimes like the phrase discussed in #3, other times on a single note. This sort of repetition heightened the intensity and rhythmic drive of the phrases in which it was used. At the beginning of the last A section of the SECOND CHORUS he repeated and emphasized the 9 of the key for nearly four measures, followed by another hint of the "Lester Leaps In" melody.

8. Repetition was again used in the opening phrase of the THIRD CHORUS (where the stop-time breaks begin), this time in very closely arranged notes (lowered 5, 5, and raised 5), in a phrase that seems to mime the sound of a bumble-bee.

9. He followed the bumble-bee phrase with a phrase that pulled into use all three of the blue notes.

10. In the second A section of the THIRD CHORUS, he began by playing two more descending phrases based on the pentatonic scale, then played a phrase that built upward in semitones, sounding "bluesy" and raising the intensity level.

11. At the B section of the THIRD CHORUS, he played a fundamental phrase (1–2–3–4–5–4–3–2–1) that may help the listener to learn what a simple digital pattern sounds like in the middle of a solo.

12. "Prez" sometimes used alternate fingerings for the single-note phrases, causing the quality to change, but not the pitch. An example of this occurred in the beginning of the last A section of the THIRD CHORUS, where he repeats the note over and over, fingering it traditionally half the time and fingering it as though it were in the lower register (but it is not) the other half of the time. The latter will sound louder than the former. This phrase is one of Young's trademarks and was widely adopted by other tenor saxophonists.

13. In the FOURTH CHORUS, the arrangement has Lester alternating four-measure segments with the pianist (Count Basie), with the pianist playing the first four measures of each formal section. In Young's first segment, he played one of his familiar blues clichés, emphasizing the lowered 7 and lowered 5.

14. In his next entrance he used a chromatically (in semi-tones) descending side-slip.

15. His next phrase, which is in the last half of the B section, is much like the phrase discussed in #6, emphasizing again the raised 5 and the 9 of the chord.

16. In the last A section of the FOURTH CHORUS, he played a slightly embellished pentatonic scale, first in a descending

phrase, then an upward one, as though he was trying to play the first phrase backward.

17. In the FIFTH CHORUS, "Prez" only had two 4-measure segments on which to solo, those being the last four measures of the first A section and the last four measures of the last A section. In his first segment he used the repeated-note approach again, this time using alternate fingerings like the idea discussed in #12, but in a higher register this time, completing the phrase with an idea nearly identical to the passage discussed in #3, again based on the lowered 7. In his last phrase, at the end of the FIFTH CHORUS, he once again plays the pentatonic scale in a descending direction. Sonny Stitt, a well-known be-bop tenor and alto saxophone player, used this phrase to create the melody to his recording of "Stitt's It," a tune which also uses the chord progression of "I Got Rhythm."

YOUNG DISCOGRAPHY

At His Very Best, Emarcy 66010

Classic Tenors, Atco FD 10146

Essential Lester Young, Verve 69398

Lester's Here, Norgran MG N-1071

Pres and His Cabinet, Verve VSPS-27

Young Lester Young, CBS, 65384

Also to be investigated:

1. Recordings made with the Count Basie Orchestra of 1936–1940.
2. Kansas City Seven recordings with Basie.
3. Two-lp collections of Basie (from the thirties) on Decca and Roulette.
4. Three selections by Young (with Basie) in the Smithsonian Collection.

CHARLES PARKER (1920–1955)
(Bird)

In this writer's opinion, as well as the opinion of many others, Charles Parker was the greatest jazz musician who ever lived. Ironically, his playing career was shorter than that of the other players covered in this chapter. Bird began making records around 1940, chiefly backing blues singers and playing with large swing orchestras like Jay McShann. But his major output really began around 1945, when, after a five-year incubation period, he and Dizzy Gillespie unveiled the be-bop style, a style which has continued to be a thriving influence for thirty-two years![3] His subsequent career was compacted into a ten-year period, ending with his death in 1955.

The 1940 recordings reveal that Bird listened to (and sounded like) altoists Buster Smith (with Jimmy Lunceford), Benny Carter, and Johnny Hodges (with Duke Ellington), as well as tenorist Lester Young. While be-bop was incubating (1940–1945), so was Bird, and by 1945 he'd left his earlier influences (with the possible exception of Buster Smith) and developed a personal style that was both unique and complete and that changed only slightly during the last ten years of his life. While it is true that Dizzy and Bird were in fact working on the stylistic ingredients of be-bop prior to 1945[4] in areas such as new scales, patterns, chord substitution, chord extensions (9th, 11th, 13th), and chord voicings, Bird's uniqueness went far beyond what was necessary to sound like a be-bop musician. Be-bop was only one facet of the Parker style. Bird was the truly consummate artist who had *everything,* and his individual greatness outshines and outlives any passing style of jazz. Placed in another time, another style, he

---

[3]At this writing there is a noticeable resurgence of interest in be-bop among very young players who previously were of the rock idiom.

[4]Parker and Gillespie, when they were both playing with the Earl "Fatha" Hines swing orchestra, were heard by Hines as they practiced backstage during intermissions, on materials that were new to jazz.

most assuredly would have achieved the same degree of greatness.[5]

The extent of Bird's influence on other jazz musicians can best be summed up in testimonies from two extraordinary jazz figures, Charles Mingus and Lennie Tristano. Mingus recorded a piece called "Gunslingin' Bird," which also bears a longer title, "If Bird Had Been a Gunslinger, There'd Be a Whole Lot of Dead Copycats." Tristano (who recorded a piece called "Requiem for Bird") once stated in an interview that Bird could have sued virtually every jazz musician for plagiarism, if the copying of improvisatory styles could be grounds for such action. Bird's sound alone has become *the* model for alto saxophonists, even those who work as fringe-area jazz musicians in dance bands, recording studios, and show bands, as lead alto players in saxophone sections.

At this point in our study, it should not surprise the reader to learn that, for all the efforts of Bird imitators (many of whom are well known), no one succeeded in duplicating the Parker style,[6] although many became famous trying, like Sonny Stitt, Phil Woods, Cannonball Adderley, Ornette Coleman, Charlie Mariano, and many other altoists. Bird's influence went beyond players of his instrument, however, being widely imitated by players of all instruments. (Bud Powell and Hampton Hawes were both influenced pianistically by Art Tatum, but both based their melodic improvisations on the Parker style.)

Bird achieved total artistry and craftsmanship of the type that would permit him to play whatever he wished. His audience knew this and hence enjoyed calling him "Bird,"

[5]In his last years Parker complained of the confinement of using chord progressions as a foundation for improvising. He was bored with the process and was seeking new horizons. He urged his disciples to listen to Stravinsky's "Le Sacre du Printemps." Just before his death, Bird sought study with avant-garde composer Ernst Krenek.

[6]It has been proven that even the layman can distinguish between Bird and Bird imitators, when solos by both are excerpted and mingled together for one listening. This can be accomplished after less than three hours of prior listening to Bird recordings.

symbolizing their awareness of his unique level of freedom, "free as a bird." The death of his spirit is rejected daily in the now familiar graffito statement, "BIRD LIVES!"

Parker's sound was probably the largest ever heard on an alto saxophone. It cannot always be taken for granted that a player's sound is large because it seems so on the recordings or even in person at a club or concert. Under those circumstances, where microphones and/or pickups are used, the balance can be adjusted with the turn of a knob. Tenorist Gene Ammons, for example, played with a very small sound but knew how to use a microphone effectively, and so his fine, if small, tone sounded big, warm, and rich in performance. You can only be sure that a sound is large if you have heard it at its acoustical (unamplified) size. This writer had such an opportunity, having heard Bird, unamplified, virtually drown out the entire Woody Herman Orchestra! It was a huge, poignantly singing sound that reached every corner and bounced off every wall of a large room.

He would have to have had ample technique to have easily coped with the very fast tempi used in the be-bop period, but the well-trained musician of any style can attest to the fact that there is more to technique than merely moving the fingers rapidly. It must be controlled, with respect to evenness, so that the player's pulse-feeling always agrees with the tempo of the accompaniment. The improviser must be able to change rhythmic levels frequently and spontaneously, without altering the tempo. Finally, the fingers must respond instantly and flawlessly to the improvisor's musical thoughts, yet *sound* fluent and relaxed, as though the phrase had been composed long ago and been played many times since then. Immature technique won't hold up to these standards, but Bird's technique made a plaything of such problems. He incorporated more rhythmic variety into his solos than any player in jazz history, before and after his time. Parker frequently played several rhythmic levels within a single, short (a measure or two) phrase, which requires thoughtfulness and musicianship, as well as technical command of the instrument.

His time-feeling was both accurate and expressive, in that he could swing explosively on bright tempi, then play a ballad or a blues in which he'd bend the tempo slightly by delaying the last few notes of a phrase, then catching up to the tempo at the very end of the phrase. This created a hesitant, naturally conversational feeling, one in which the storyteller slows and speeds the pace of the words for emphasis and/or expression at certain points.

Parker exhibited masterful control of his tonal materials. He floated deftly through all keys, treating each as though it were the key of C. He understood the exact effect of every note of every chord in the progression, surprising you frequently with beautiful notes you hadn't anticipated or wouldn't have imagined without his help. If he became momentarily bored with the progression, he'd superimpose a substitute chord or play both the assigned chord and the substitute chord. Bird transformed the four-chord bridge of "I Got Rhythm" into a sixteen-chord progression, over the same eight-measure duration. In addition to understanding and using all tonal materials available, he could also instantly recognize and respond to the sound of any chord and/or progression *by ear,* when it became necessary (when sitting in with another group, for instance).

His spirit/drive was at least equal to that of Armstrong, though Bird seldom played solos, even long ones, in which the intensity level continues to rise throughout the solo. But his cleverness and singing quality, prevalent throughout all his solos, prevent the listener from becoming too aware of a lack of anything. Despite the number of flighty phrases contained in a given solo, even ballads, Parker was an intensely lyrical improviser, one of the few who could use quicker phrases to embellish a melodious solo without sacrificing the main thrust of his melodies.

Bird's repertoire included mostly blues, standard tunes,

be-bop tunes, and ballads. His specific choices of tunes within those categories were sometimes discerning (i.e., "The Song Is You," "Round Midnite," "Just Friends," and "Sippin' at Bell's"), and at other times the choices seemed random or hasty (i.e., a profusion of "I Got Rhythm"-based tunes, tunes without melody choruses, arbitrarily-chosen blues, etc.). In other words, he knew the difference between an average tune and a great one, but he also knew that most any vehicle would suffice as a setting for his improvisations, as he was extremely versatile, sounding comfortable and inspired on all vehicles available to him. Parker also expressed his versatility in terms of various kinds of groups, recording with be-bop combos, big bands (swing and be-bop), strings, blues singers, Latin bands, Jazz at the Philharmonic groups (concerts in the manner of a jam session), and voices (Dave Lambert Singers.)

Parker's innovative strength has already been discussed, with respect to his early influences, the incubation period for both Bird and the style of be-bop (1940–1945), and his awesome influence upon virtually all jazz musicians. Perhaps it is now easier for the reader to understand why many jazz musicians and jazz historians consider Charles Parker to be the consummate master of jazz improvisation, as he has no weaknesses in the evaluative criteria. In fact, he is distinctively strong in *every* aspect.

CHARLES PARKER on "Don't Blame Me" *(Spotlite 10)*

vehicle type:	Standard
formal structure:	AABA (32 measures)
arrangement:	4-bar introduction (trumpet and rhythm)
	1 chorus alto saxophone solo
	8-bar trumpet solo (an "A" section)

Selecting a single Parker solo for study was difficult. He was a great blues player, a standout on very bright tempi, and one of the most sensitive ballad players in jazz. Furthermore, he never really played a weak, uninspired solo. Even during the recording of "Lover Man" (1947), when he suffered a complete physical and mental collapse from drugs, he was poignantly expressive on each of the widely separated phrases. He got considerable support from Jimmy Bunn (the pianist), who, after playing a lovely, inspired introduction, watched over Bird protectively throughout the selection, filling in for him whenever he was unable to play the next phrase. The decision to use a ballad for study rested on the fact that Bird generally played ballads more spontaneously and focused on beauty. In brighter tempi and blues, he was subject to incorporationg more change-running ideas, typical Parker clichés, humorous quotes from other tunes, and the like, all of which are fun to hear. But if we have only one Parker selection for study, a ballad will yield more beauty. Other selections considered for study and highly recommended for listening are "Embraceable You," "Out of Nowhere," "Now's the Time" (blues), "I Remember You," "Just Friends," and "Dark Shadows" (blues). It would also be interesting to compare the 1940 versions of "Lady Be Good" and "Cherokee" with the versions of those tunes released 6-12 years later. "Don't Blame Me," however, does contain many of Bird's most musical traits.

Analysis/Annotations

1. Listen to the chords of the introduction, a typical progression that contains elements used by Parker in other progressions. The trumpet player, incidentally, is the very young Miles Davis.

2. Note the tempo. Be-boppers not only used faster tempi, generally, than had been used in prior jazz styles, but they also slowed the tempo more for ballads. Compare, for example, the difference between this tempo ("Don't Blame Me") and the tempo taken by Hawkins on "How Deep Is the Ocean" or

"Body and Soul." Swing era players were influenced by their profession of playing for dancers, probably, where they grew accustomed to hearing ballads played fast enough to inspire dancers of a particular style. As be-bop was never conceived to be dance music, the ballad could be slowed to a musically appropriate, if undanceable, pace.

3. Because of the slower ballad tempo, the 78 rpm record on which it was first issued was only able to accommodate one full chorus plus the introduction and Miles' "extra" "A" section solo, a grand total of only 44 measures. Therefore Bird could not afford to devote a full chorus, or even eight measures, to the given melody. This practice of omitting the given melody, or only suggesting it loosely, was begun in the swing period. Hawkins did it frequently, and legendary trombonist Jack Jenny once recorded one of the greatest solos of all time on two choruses of "Stardust" without once suggesting the given melody. Tragically, Jenny died very young, and the record was never reissued. An eight-measure Jenny solo on "Stardust" survived, however, that was recorded when he was with the Artie Shaw Orchestra. As Bird only suggests the given melody enough times to indicate that he knows and inwardly hears the melody, it would be helpful to listen first to another recording of the tune, so that *you* will know when he is alluding to a fragment of the melody.

4. Parker's first entrance, just ahead of the first beat of the chorus, is a typical example of the Bird "in flight." His objective is the tonic (1) or keynote, which he plays on the downbeat (first beat) of the chorus. As the last chord of the introduction is a favorite harmonic cliché of Bird's,[7] he doubtlessly couldn't resist the opportunity to use that chord as a rich setting for his rapid, highly embellished entrance.

5. After arriving on the keynote, on the first beat of the chorus, Parker pauses briefly, then plays seven notes, mostly in an ascending direction, which loosely describe the melody. To illustrate how an improviser can embellish a melody without leaving it altogether, the seven pitches are numbered with

[7]Called *tri-tone substitution.*

underscores to indicate which are the three notes of the given melody's first phrase:

$$1-2-\underline{3}-4-\underline{5}-6-\underline{7}$$

(these numbers in no way indicate the function of the notes with their given chord, as was done earlier wtih digital patterns).

6. After another pause, he again suggests the melody in a four-note phrase (descending in semi-tones) in which only the second and fourth notes are the melody notes.

7. At this point (the third measure of the chorus), Bird departs from the melody entirely for the remainder of the first "A" section, playing instead quick phrases that focus on aspects of the chords and the progression. Note that the quick phrase of the third measure is played again in the fifth measure, where the same chord recurs as well. As an example of Parker's extraordinary rhythmic diversity, consider this list of the various rhythmic levels investigated by him in the first "A" section alone:

In terms of interesting notes, during the six measures of swift phrases, he used three 9ths, three raised 5ths, four lowered 9ths, and one raised 9th, each contributing to the overall richness of his harmonies.

8. The last flurry of the first "A" section continues across the dividing line between the "A" sections, spilling into the first couple of beats of the second "A" section. This is a good example of *overlapping,* discussed earlier.

9. The flurry mentioned in #8 ends on a longer note (3rd beat of first measure of the second "A" section) that happens to be the first melody note of that section, arriving two beats late. Again he implied the melody's first three-note phrase in an embellished form. This time the first note of the melody is the last note of an improvised phrase that began in the previous eight-measure segment, arriving two beats late, followed by a new and flighty phrase that *ends* with the second and third notes of the given melody. So he began two beats late, yet managed to work in another flurry while catching up!

10. After catching up to the given melody, Bird paused, then played exactly the same phrase mentioned in #6, which was at the same point within the identical "A" sections.

11. The last six measures of the second "A" section were handled very much like the last six measures of the first "A," a series of short flurries, a total absence of the given melody, and some interesting, if buried, note choices.

12. Note that he also played a nearly identical phrase in the first two beats of the seventh measure in both "A" sections. As mentioned in Chapter 4, improvisers tend to form the habit of hearing or playing similar phrases in like places.

13. Listen to the manner in which Parker slowed the rhythmic motion in the last measure before the bridge, where he then returned to the slower-moving given melody.

14. At "B" (the bridge), he played the first four notes of the given melody, played an embellishing flurry for the remainder of that measure (where the fourth note of the given melody is sustained), then returns to play the next four notes of the given melody. After still another quick improvised phrase he outlined the two melody notes that occur over the third and fourth measures of the bridge, in the midst of his flight.

15. In the fourth measure of the bridge, Bird played a typical example of the pulse-delaying effect at ends of phrases mentioned in the discussion about his time-feeling.

16. Parker improvised almost exclusively on one fast rhythmic level (32nd notes) for measures five and six of the bridge, one of his busiest segments.

17. The last two measures of the bridge is the most strikingly beautiful part of the entire solo. The four-chord progression used in those two measures, first of all, is not the given progression. It is a dramatic, colorful substitute progression, used by Bird in a number of other recordings (often highlighting those solos, also), and he probably felt the same inspiration in this progression as he seemingly felt in the last bar of the introduction, where he responded to the inviting *tri-tone substitution* there. Observe how differently he approached that long phrase of the last two measures of the bridge. He slowed the rhythmic motion abruptly, "raised his voice" (played with more deliberation and emphasis), "cleared his throat" (brightened his sound), went into the upper register, then descended on the wings of some very choice notes to a natural tapered phrase ending. It is the lyrical climax of the solo, and those two measures alone would make the recording worth many repeated listenings. That segment illustrates what was meant in Chapter 4 (discussion of originality) by "the creative heart of the solo."

18. At the beginning of the last "A" section (after the bridge), Parker alluded briefly to the given melody for the last time, improvising freely after the first five beats, during which he implied the first three melody notes in much the same way as at the beginning of the chorus.

19. Listen again for rhythmic variety during the remainder of the last eight measures. There are at least as many rhythmic levels as cited in #7. Notice, too, that he used space (rests) very well. Silence is effective as part of a rhythmic effect, when it is surrounded on both ends by sound. It is also an effective tool for delineating between phrases.

20. In the sixth measure of the last eight-measure segment of Bird's chorus, he played a one-measure phrase that almost equals the one discussed in #17. It ascends, then descends in a pretty way, sounding lyrical, dramatic, and fancifully embellished. This time he responded to a pretty progression that is

used as a point of drama in many *standard* tune progressions, instead of a progression invented during the be-bop period.

21. The solo ends with another example of the Parker trait mentioned in the discussion of his time, and again in #15, in which he delayed the pulse of the first few notes, in a halting manner, then worked his way downward to a good final note, catching up to the tempo as he went, so that the final note arrived on time.

After that, Miles Davis played a stunning eight-measure solo, from the standpoint of note choices and lyricism, qualities for which he is well known.

PARKER DISCOGRAPHY

Bird Is Free, Charlie Parker PLP-401

Charles Christopher Parker, Jr.: Bird/The Savoy Recordings, Savoy SJL 2201 (multivolume set)

Charlie Parker Story, Vols. 1, 2, and *3,* Verve 8000, 8001, 8002

Early Bird, Baronet B-107

Essential Charlie Parker, Verve 8409

Genius of Charlie Parker, Vols. 1–8, Verve 8003–8010

Greatest Jazz Concert Ever, Prestige 24024 (2 record set)

(plus seven selections by Parker in the Smithsonian Collection)

MILES DAVIS (1926–   )

Miles Davis' career is one of the most fascinating and unique stories in all of jazz history. He has been a well-known jazz figure for many years, but the reasons for his unparalleled success are very different from, say, Armstrong's or

Parker's. Miles didn't take the jazz world by storm in a smashing debut, although his career began at age 20 as a member of the Parker Quintet. Many musicians wondered why Bird selected him to be in his illustrious group. The younger set of trumpet players who felt that Bird must have known what he was doing blindly went about imitating young Miles. But very few of them knew the exact nature of Miles' musical gift, and so they imitated him in the most superficial manner, taking to playing with a dead, flat sound, and developing a technique that could be called "studied sloppiness." They draped their fingers languidly over the trumpet valves, so that they weren't using the more controlled tips of the fingers, and they did what they could to look and sound totally relaxed at all times. Indeed, if you weren't listening very carefully, you might have agreed with his imitators in their superficial assessment, whether or not you liked his playing. Miles did sound unusually relaxed (even when he wasn't), he played without a vibrato, had a relatively dead (but fat and pretty at times) sound, and used quick, short *grace notes*[8] before longer notes that created an effect that some might have thought to be sloppiness. He wasn't considered, by many trumpet players, to have much instrumental ability either. His range was quite small, his sound was unpolished and small, he seemed to have flat intonation,[9] and he didn't show much finger agility.

Miles had to *win* his audience with a style that was unfamiliar (as he didn't sound like anyone before him), a technique that was questionable to many, and a personality that wasn't exactly out of Dale Carnegie.[10] An audience of the forties didn't have to put up with that, because there were players around like Dizzy Gillespie and Louis Armstrong,

[8]*Grace notes* are very short notes, usually a semi-tone below the note to follow, rhythmically placed as close to the next note as possible.

[9]Keep in mind that Bird played *extremely* sharp, which inexplicable trait may have caused Miles to sound flatter than he really was.

[10]Miles was notorious for turning his back to an audience, walking offstage when he wasn't playing (while the performance continued), and being cool to interviewers.

with their musical and personal dynamism. But the few musicians and listeners who refused to believe that Bird's selection of Miles was haphazard or mistaken searched for Miles' true musical qualities and found them to be ample, though not in the same areas mentioned thus far. Through Miles, they discovered purity, economy, originality, and lyricism in music. But that was only the beginning. He became an astute judge of talent, fostering the musical growth of many young players, relatively unknown at the time, who became giants while playing in Miles' groups. Such a list would include John Coltrane, Chick Corea, Ron Carter, Tony Williams, Herbie Hancock, George Coleman, Airto Moreira, Paul Chambers, Wayne Shorter, Red Garland, Philly Joe Jones, Joe Zawinul, John McLaughlin, Wynton Kelly, Jimmy Cobb, and Bennie Maupin!

Those who were not convinced of Davis' musical strengths in 1945, when he was playing with Parker, became convinced eventually, nonetheless. They were converted by recordings like the semi-big band of 1949–1950 *(Birth of the Cool)* or "Walkin' " (1954), or "Round Midnight" (1957), or one of the *third stream*[11] albums with Gil Evans, like *Sketches of Spain* (1960). Sooner or later, he won them over.

Not that Miles wasn't already a great player in 1945, but he did in fact improve over the years, both as a trumpet player and an improviser. His sound became large, fat, and expressive. His range expanded enormously and he utilized it more of the time for variety and impact. His control of the horn developed to the point that in "Saeta" *(Sketches of Spain)* Miles exhibits his ability to slide evenly from one pitch to another without a mechanical break in sound, to color the qualities of individual notes of the phrase in very expressive ways, to have sustained notes sail upward *(doit)* or downward

---

[11]In the middle fifties an attempt was made by Gil Evans, Gunther Schuller, John Lewis, J.J. Johnson, George Russell and others (all composers) to write long, concerto-like pieces (often showcasing Miles) for something resembling a symphony orchestra or an oversized jazz band, in which the style would approximate a cross between jazz and classical music. Schuller coined the term, "third-stream music."

(fall-off) at the very end, and to create a sort of sobbing sound that alludes to the Spanish singer on the balcony above a solemn, religious parade, singing of the agonies of the Crucifixion. His technique, in terms of speed and agility, also became more pronounced. There were increases in melodic form, shaping of phrases, rhythmic diversity, conviction, angularity, and even some humor in his improvisations. He also changed or modified his style several times. Trumpet players who would imitate Miles have to remain flexible and abreast of his most recent output, because Miles is never standing still. He has become the fashion plate of jazz, and that is his most significant contribution of all. Miles has set the tone of jazz for more than thirty years, being partly or entirely responsible for virtually every nuance that has changed the sound of jazz since 1945! No one, not even Armstrong or Parker, has accomplished such a feat. Consider the changes he has brought about. They include instrumentation (accessory percussion, bass clarinet, electric keyboards, synthesizer, electronic gadgetry, and the use of multiple keyboards), new players (already listed), style (the merging of jazz with rock, be-bop, free-form, third stream), and countless other innovations (use of coloristic devices, side-slipping, outside playing, longer solos and selections, and the reversal of horn and rhythm section function, as in "Nefertiti"). Miles has almost single-handedly kept jazz in a state of continuous change and evolution from 1945 to the present.

Because Miles has a complex, ever-changing style, it was necessary, while describing him, to integrate our appreciative criteria (sound, technique, time, etc.) into that description. The only criterion not covered was his use of tonal materials. It was mentioned that he used economy, side-slipping, outside playing, and the like, which gives some indications, but little was said about his note choices, which are vital to his musical thrust. Even in 1945, Miles was already hearing with a uniquely discriminating ear. There was a certain purity about it (and still is) that told the listener that Miles wasn't going to play anything in a redundant, insincere, wasteful manner. Every note had to pass inspection in the mind, in the ear, and in his musical taste buds. If he heard nothing, momentarily, he played nothing, waiting for a better idea. He could not be hurried or forced to play anything that did not measure to up his standards. If one had the opportunity to study very carefully a progression on which Miles was to improvise subsequently, and if that person were to circle the very best notes available in each chord or scale, crossing out all notes which would have little effect, the version played by Miles would probably include only those better notes, except that he would probably hear a few that weren't circled or crossed out.

Another distinction, with regard to Davis' note choices, is that he doesn't bother to harmonically justify a note that is already known to be richly effective, even if it is remote from the basic sound of the given chord. To explain, suppose a player decides to play a raised-9 against a certain chord. Most players would precede or embellish such a remote, colorful note with a few other tones (like 3 and 7, for example) that would clarify, aurally, the relationship of the raised-9 to the more fundamental notes of the chord. But Miles is likely, under the same circumstances, simply to play the raised-9 by itself or juxtapose it with a fundamental note that is perhaps a semi-tone away (like the 3rd of the chord, which when placed in the same octave as the raised-9th, would be a semi-tone higher), or even introduce one or two other remote, colorful notes along wtih the raised-9, not bothering to justify those, either! In other words, Miles will play it, but he won't explain it. That's the listener's problem.

The 1976 edition of the Schwann Catalog lists thirty-five albums by Miles Davis. Within that span were several style changes, many innovations, and many great groups. A selection for study and analysis, then, was somewhat arbitrary. "Straight, No Chaser" (from *Milestones,* Columbia CS 9498, 1958) was selected for several reasons. It is a blues (by Thelonious Monk) that is very basic to jazz, distinctive, yet familiar to the average listener; also, we haven't analyzed a blues performance up to now. The group personnel is one of his best (Coltrane, Adderly, Garland, Chambers, and Jones), the album was popular among musicians, and it is a reasonably typical sample of Miles' playing about halfway through his career. No single selection will reveal his total contribution, however, since he is ever-changing.

MILES DAVIS on "Straight, No Chaser" *(Columbia CS 9498)*

vehicle type:	blues
formal structure:	12 measures
arrangement:	Davis' eight-chorus solo is between the Adderly and Coltrane solos.

Analysis/Annotations

1. Listen to the last phrase played by Adderly, which spilled into Miles' first chorus, and which Miles then took up and developed for the first eight measures of the chorus. The idea fed to Miles by Adderly was not new to Miles. It is a quote from a blues tune by Bird, called "Au Privave," recorded years earlier when Miles played with Bird.

2. An example of the oft-imitated grace notes, mentioned earlier, happens in the ninth and tenth measures of the first chorus.

3. The opening phrase of the second chorus sounds like an embellished version of "When the Saints Go Marching In," which may have planted a seed, as it crops up again later. The phrase is hard to catch here, as he continued building a line after the implied quote.

4. The line that follows the implied quote is filled with trademarks of the Davis style of the middle fifties, the style he played on "Walkin' " in 1954.

5. Listen to the half-valved "blue" (♭3) in the fifth measure of the second chorus (which sounds much like a short *squeeze*). Then in the seventh measure, he played a "blue" 5th (♭5),

this time coloring the sound with a *fall-off*, giving the note a sassy feeling.

6. The opening phrase of the third chorus is a quote from "Anything You Can Do, I Can Do Better," a popular song of the day; then in the middle of the phrase it becomes a quote from a very similar tune of the forties, called "Scatterbrain."

7. In the ninth measure of the third chorus, Miles sustained a "surprise" note, then ran quickly up a scale. What he actually did was to lower the 5 of that particular chord (the note he sustained at the bottom, before running up the scale). Then, because he slightly changed the chord, a different scale could be used with the chord, namely the *lydian augmented scale,* an invention of George Russel whose new system of tonal organization had just been touted by Miles in a Downbeat magazine interview. That was the quick scale he played in the ninth measure.

8. The third chorus ends with a "blue" 3, embellished by another sassy fall-off.

9. The fourth chorus begins with another implied quote from "Saints," this time much closer to that melody.

10. In the fifth measure of the fourth chorus, Miles began an eight-measure development of a very simple idea, moving it around in much the manner of an early rock-and-roll bass line. Listen to the manner in which he colored the last note of that chorus, so typical of Miles.

11. The first eight measures of the fifth chorus is given to a very exacting quote of "Saints" and successive variations.

12. Beginning in the ninth measure of the fifth chorus, Miles began a series of three similar phrases, with the third one jumping to a higher note and continuing over the dividing line between choruses *(overlapping)*, a device of which Miles was a master. On the way down from the high note he used two half-valve notes.

13. After descending from the just-mentioned high note, he ascended on another unusual scale in the third measure of the sixth chorus, called the *diminished scale,* which contains two of the three blue notes, the lowered 3 and 5.

14. Perhaps as a result of the diminished scale, he spent the re-

mainder of the sixth chorus and the entire seventh chorus emphasizing the "blue" 3 and 5 repeating the diminished scale in the ninth measure of the seventh chorus.

15. One last mild allusion to "Saints" was played at the beginning of the eighth (and last) chorus, lasting about four measures.

16. In the fourth measure of the eighth chorus, listen to the idea played by the pianist (Red Garland) in the background, then note how Miles picked up on the idea, playing it in the fifth measure.

17. He followed that idea by raising the highest note a semi-tone, sliding up to the pitch to great effect.

18. The last two notes of Davis' solo, spilling into Coltrane's first chorus, are the lowered 5 and a 9 (surprising choices). Trane then began his solo on the 9, echoing Miles, then resolved the note to the keynote (1) in the bluesy, embellished manner.

DAVIS DISCOGRAPHY

Agharta, Columbia PG-33967 (2 records)

At Carnegie Hall, Col. PC-8612

At Fillmore, Col, CG-30038 (2 records)

Basic Miles, Col. KC-32025

Big Fun, Col. PG-32886 (2 records)

Bitches Brew, Col. PG-26 (2 records)

Blue Moods, Fantasy 86001

Conception, Prestige 7744

ESP, Col. PC-9150

Facets, CBS 62637

Filles de Kilimanjaro, Col. PC-9750

Four and More, Col. PC-9253

Get Up with It, Col. PG-33236 (2 records)

Greatest Hits, Col. PC-9808

In a Silent Way, Col. PC-9875

In Concert, Col. PG-32092 (2 records)

In Europe, Col. PC-8983

In Person at the Blackhawk, Col. C2S-820 (2 records)

Jazz at the Plaza, Vol. 1, Col. PC-32470

Kind of Blue, Col. PC-8163

Live Evil, Col. CG-30954 (2 records)

Miles Ahead, Col. PC-8633

Miles Davis, Prestige 24001

Miles Davis, United Artists 9952

Miles in the Sky, Col. PC-9628

Miles Smiles, Col. PC-9401

Milestones, Col. PC-9428

My Funny Valentine, Col. PC-9106

Nefertiti, Col. KCS-9594

Oleo, Prestige 7847

On the Corner, Col. KC-31906

Porgy and Bess, Col. PC-8085

Quiet Nights, Col. PC-8906

'Round about Midnight, Col. PC-8649

Seven Steps to Heaven, Col. PC-8851

Sketches of Spain, Col. PC-8271

Someday My Prince Will Come, Col. PC-8456

Sorceress, Col. PC-9532

Tribute to Jack Johnson, Col. KC-30455

Walkin', Prestige 7608

JOHN COLTRANE (1926–1967)
(Trane)

The life of John Coltrane bears a strong resemblance to the tale "The Red Shoes," in which a young woman who loves to dance is helplessly drawn to purchasing a pair of hexed red shoes from a warlock-like shoemaker. When she puts on the shoes, she is compelled to dance vigorously and joyously; and when she tires, the red shoes will not permit her to stop dancing, not even long enough to take off the shoes, and so she dances to exhaustion and death. Trane's exhaustive efforts in music were legendary, apparent both in practice and performance. He was observed on one occasion, in the height of his career, to have practiced exclusively the "C" major scale for eleven straight hours, not even stopping to eat or rest! His recordings tell much the same tale, with the long, long solos at an intensity level that was almost superhuman, greater than any player in history. It is entirely possible that those tremendous outlays of energy shortened his life. Jazz musicians are not physical pansies, or they couldn't really play. To play the instrument at an intensity level approaching Trane's level is a physical workout in itself, taxing the muscles of the lips, face, throat, chest, stomach, back, arms, fingers, and even the legs. One long, intense solo like Trane's can bring about any or all of the following conditions, sometimes after the end of the solo: (1) heavy breathing, (2) drenching perspiration, (3) trembling, (4) nausea (from tensing stomach muscles to drive air through the horn, not, it is hoped, nausea from nervousness or because of the quality of the solo), (5) uncontrollable exhilaration, (6) fatigue, (7) depression, and (8) muscular tension (residual) and soreness. Add to all that the other kinds of stress and strain, like emotional stress (the pressure of being watched, listened to, and recorded; the excitement of the creation; and the strain of phrasing the music with intense expression, dynamics, swells, etc.) and mental strain (concentration on form, changes, aesthetic judgements; translation of thoughts into notes and fingerings; listening to the accompaniment; etc.). If we could measure the energy level for a given duration, say, for one 32-measure chorus by each artist, and then measure and compare Trane's energy output to that of Lester Young, for example, Trane's level would probably be somewhere between five and ten times greater. That doesn't necessarily mean that he is a better player than Young, but merely indicates an expenditure of more energy. Also consider that after that first 32-measure chorus, Prez will probably have gone on to perhaps one or two more choruses, while Trane might continue for twenty or thirty more choruses.

Leonard Feather[12] notes:

> Around '61 Coltrane became involved in the Indian improvisational concept, which entailed lengthy improvisations often based on a predetermined mode (scale arrangement) rather than on chords. Tremendous emotional vitality was transmitted on his recordings (particularly *Africa/Brass, At the Village Vanguard,* and *Impressions*). Some critics attacked his use of harsh, human sounds and his often excessively long solos as "honking and bleating" and "anti-jazz," and claimed that his playing was sheer technical display that was without musical value and was destructive to jazz. Nevertheless, this innovation of Indian and modal ideas led to greater freedom for jazz soloists in the '60s, taking the music away from improvisations on songs or song patterns and allowing it to move toward a wholly new musical feeling. At the same time he recorded several blues numbers and two LPs devoted to ballads, with a combination of sensitivity and intensity that have come to characterize all of his efforts.

A doctor specializing in sleep cure (in which an exhausted patient is placed under sedation in a special hospital for a period of one to three months, for rejuvenation purposes) was once interviewed for a magazine article. He was asked what group of people most often used his services, to which he replied that his patients were mostly actors and actresses, show business people, and socialites. When asked if they needed it, he responded in the negative, saying that their work and their lifestyle give them ample opportunity to release tensions. The reporter then asked what group of people probably needed it most, to which he replied, "the jazz musician." He felt that the pressures are excessive for a

---

[12]*The Encyclopedia of Jazz in the Sixties,* Leonard Feather, Horizon Press, New York, 1966.

person improvising music for an audience or a recording, and the preparation can be rushed and intense.

Trane, in his early twenties, was playing with Dizzy Gillespie and Charles Parker in the late forties but he remained unnoticed until he joined Miles Davis in 1956. During the several years spent with Miles, Trane was chiefly a change-running player with considerable techniques. The influences would seem to have been Bird, Sonny Stitt, and Sonny Rollins. His sound didn't have the drive of later years, and his note choices were routinely and arbitrarily chosen, for the most part. This change-running stage of his career reached a sensational culminating point in the 1959 album, *Giant Steps*, with his own group.

In the meantime he had made the *Kind Of Blue* album with Miles, which introduced Trane (and everyone else) to modal tunes. Two years later, in 1961, Coltrane recorded "Impressions," a modal tune with the same changes as "So What" (from *Kind of Blue*), along with modal treatments of tunes like "My Favorite Things," "Out of This World," and "Chim Chim Cheree" (all standard tunes with a new interpretation). This is the phase of his career discussed in the Leonard Feather excerpt. It is also during these years (1960–1965) that Trane acquired his outstanding rhythm section, with McCoy Tyner on piano, Jimmy Garrison on bass, and Elvin Jones on drums, and the period in which he begins to play soprano saxophone on some selections. That period ends in 1965, with the climaxing album, *A Love Supreme*, which is a modal album (dedicated to God) that uses a three-note motive and its endless variations as the exclusive melodic material for the entire album.

After *A Love Supreme*, Trane launches into still another phase, which is largely made up of free-form pieces, experiments in instrumentation (like *Interstellar Space*, a duo of Trane and drummer Rashied Ali), blistering technique, the introduction of new and unusual players (i.e., Ali, Archie Shepp, Pharoah Sanders, and Alice Coltrane), and a continuation of modal and Eastern musical concepts.

Trane's sound was extremely full and hard. Some listeners found it objectionable, but there are few tenor saxophonists today who don't allude to that sound. His technique was phenomenally swift, beyond even Parker's fine technique. His time was very emphatic and accurate, even in the brightest of tempi. His handling of tonal materials was completely thorough, masterful, and creative. In spirit/drive Trane had no equal, though he may have burned himself out with that energetic drive. Lyricism was not a very pronounced aspect of his playing from 1955 to 1960, during the change-running period, but after that Trane becomes more of a lyrical player than anything else. His repertoire included every kind of tune, though there were few contemporary tunes. Most of his output was in modal tunes, plus a reasonable number of blues, be-bop, standard, and free-form tunes. His vehicular versatility was strong, and he went through some style changes, but versatility was not actually one of his strongest points. His ballads are less appropriately handled (a little harsh), though they are certainly enjoyable, and he always sounded the same, in spite of the setting. John Coltrane was certainly an obvious innovator in many ways who exerted great influence on the succeeding generation of players.

"Acknowledgement" and "Pursuance" have been selected for study and analysis. Both tracks are from *A Love Supreme.* Two selections were chosen instead of one so that the listener can become acquainted with the three-note motive that organizes the album. "Acknowledgement" is slow, and the motive is played in a simple fashion with many repeats and variations. "Pursuance" is very fast, and though it contains many playings of the motive, it is more difficult to recognize them at the faster tempo. Therefore, it is hoped that by listening to "Acknowledgement" first, the listener may be better able to cope with "Pursuance."

JOHN COLTRANE on "Acknowledgement" *(Impulse S-77)*

vehicle type:	modal
formal structure:	not structured in measure groups
arrangement:	sustained chord with tenor cadenza
	bass announcement of motive and tempo
	drums, then piano entrance on vamp
	tenor improvisation
	voice chant
	bass ending

1. The opening cadenza played by Trane, over a sustained, rolling chord built with fourth and fifth intervals, is like an announcement or convocation. Trane used only three notes, B, E, and F# (not the theme), which supports and agrees with the sustained chord, which is a sort of E major chord.

2. When this brief segment ended, the bassist (Garrison) then played the *Love Supreme* motive as an ostinato (an indefinitely repeated figure), changing the key to F minor, remaining on that chord until the end of the vocal chant. The motive actually contains four notes (A-Love-Su-preme), but as the first and third notes of the phrase are the same, only three different pitches are used.

3. Trane entered, after a short rhythmic vamp, playing much as he did on the cadenza, though in a different key now. By emphasizing C, F, and G, then F, B♭, and C against the F minor accompaniment (alternating between the two 3-note phrases) he duplicated the effect of the cadenza with two like phrases that fit the new key. It is probable that this segment was a semi-planned melody, or if, the reader can imagine such a thing, a spontaneously created given melody. An analysis of the first eight measures shows it to be much like an "A" section's melody of a tune:

(A)

(2 measures)	(2 measures)	(2 measures)	(2 measures)
melodic phrase, based on the six notes given above	variation of six-note melody	another variation of that melody	a contrasting, closing phrase

This is a very common melodic structure, found in countless tunes from any source. Only the motives are different. Several more interesting points surface here. The contrasting phrase of the last two measures begins with the melody to "Pursuance," like a sneak preview of the next selection while functioning as a closing phrase for "Acknowledgement." The melody to "Pursuance" is a variation of the *Love Supreme* motive, which was played by Garrison at the beginning of "Acknowledgement," and by chanting voices later in the track (see illustration).

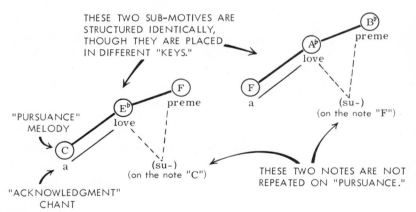

THESE TWO SUB-MOTIVES ARE STRUCTURED IDENTICALLY, THOUGH THEY ARE PLACED IN DIFFERENT "KEYS."

"PURSUANCE" MELODY

"ACKNOWLEDGMENT" CHANT

THESE TWO NOTES ARE NOT REPEATED ON "PURSUANCE."

Finally, this same pattern is repeated for the *next* eight measures, though with a different closing phrase, so that the first sixteen measures forms one sixteen-measure *chorus* of an extemporaneous (probably) modal tune, having a form of A-A or A-A'.

4. Trane definitely launched into a freer improvisation at the seventeenth measure, as though he had finished stating a

given melody, but the sixteen-measure structure soon disappeared, though fragments of the melody were incorporated into the improvising.

5. Starting from the seventeenth measure, Trane played sixteen measures of relaxed melodic material, based on the two pentatonic scales that he adopted for tonal materials throughout this selection. There were a couple of times during that sixteen measures when he sketchily implied the "Acknowledgement," *Love Supreme,* and "Pursuance" motives, but he had not yet decided to work them over thoroughly.

6. After the sixteen measures just described, Trane was warmed to the task and began a full-scale investigation of the "Pursuance" motive. This continued for some while, as he took the motive through many keys and side-slips. By this time the sixteen-measure divisions had completely been abandoned and Tyner (pianist) had begun to treat the given chord (the *only* given chord for the whole solo) more freely, indulging in much side-slipping.

7. After some time of playing variations on the "Pursuance" motive, he left it and sounded as though he might have been winding down the solo, descending in range and beginning to repeat typical closing phrases. At this point he began to work with two motives simultaneously, the "Acknowledgement" and "Pursuance" motives.

8. During the pre-mentioned section, he rose in range again and descended again, this time remaining in the lower range for a while, playing more closing phrases, as if he were sending a signal to the rest of the group that he was ready to enter a new section—and he did.

9. The new section became a series of variations on the *Love Supreme* motive, again including many transpositions into various keys, some fitting the given harmony, some not, and Tyner continued to increase the pace and scope of his side-slipping, so that the whole section has a sort of floating tonality. At the end of that section, Trane began playing the motive repeatedly in the original key (F minor), signalling his exit.

10. The vocal chant then entered, keeping the motive in F minor for a while, then it was mysteriously (and sloppily) but delib-

erately transposed to one tone lower (E♭ minor), where it remained for the remainder of the selection. The only hint of why they decided to move into E♭ minor is that the track "Resolution" (same album) is pitched in that key.

JOHN COLTRANE on "Pursuance" *(Impulse S-77)*

vehicle type:	minor blues, almost modal
formal structure:	12-measure choruses
arrangement:	long drum solo
	2 choruses of melody (24 measures)
	piano solo
	tenor solo
	2 choruses of melody
	drums and bass epilogue
	bass solo

1. After Elvin Jones' dynamic solo-introduction, Trane played two 12-measure choruses of the melody, a melody which now will, we hope, sound very familiar to the listener, as Trane worked with the "Pursuance" motive for a considerably long time in "Acknowledgement."

2. Although McCoy Tyner's brilliant, formful, and inspiring piano solo is not the topic of our analysis, his contribution cannot be ignored entirely. At least take notice of: (a) his dedication to and masterful handling and retaining of the "Pursuance" motive; (b) the many and various side-slips; and (c) the magnificent, fanfare-like last chorus that created a dramatic rise in intensity, announcing Trane's steamy entrance.

3. It takes courage to *enter* a solo at a high intensity level, since it allows no time to warm up to the project and creates the danger that there couldn't be much room in which to raise the level further, as the solo continues. but this is how Trane entered his solo, with Tyner's build-up, a heavy rhythm section, an opening high note that is only three semi-tones from the top of the horn's natural range (though Trane frequently plays above that), and playing very close to full volume and

intensity. Remarkably, the intensity curve *does* rise, in spite of all that, which is accomplished in part by increasing the number of notes (rise in density), using very high notes, near the peak of the solo, and increase in singing quality toward the latter part of the solo, using the motive in dramatic ways, outside playing and side-slipping (withheld until well into the solo), a rise in emotion, and a continued increase in density and volume in the rhythm section, particularly drums.

4. Trane played eighteen choruses of a minor blues for his solo, the last two choruses being a return of the melody choruses. For the listener, it may be too difficult to keep up with the counting of those choruses, though, as the tempo is fast and the harmonic treatment very free. It is to Trane's credit that he was able to play so freely himself, against an equally free accompaniment, without once losing his place. Often in the solo he deliberately overlapped the dividing line between choruses, but whenever he wanted to play a positive sort of melody that needed to start on the downbeat of a chorus, he was able to do so with seemingly little effort.

5. Trane opens his solo with the second fragment of the "Acknowledgement" melody and continued to develop that idea for the first three choruses. There is one brief 3-note fragment of the "Pursuance" melody in the midst of those three choruses. The nonmotivic parts of the solo, where he seemed to be running up and down some chord or scale, are *all* based on one pentatonic scale, an excellent choice, as it fits the entire minor blues progression and it contains all the notes and intervals of the *Love Supreme,* "Acknowledgement," and "Pursuance" motives (all very closely interrelated)!

6. At the beginning of the fourth chorus, where he ascended into the stratosphere for the first time, he still retained the pentatonic scale, resisting the side-slipping suggestions to prevalent in Tyner's playing during that chorus and the next. Instead, Trane descended in range and continued playing in the manner of the first three choruses.

7. Finally, about halfway through his fifth chorus, Trane succumbed to the urge to join Tyner in his urge to side-slip. So the notes of the first *four and one-half choruses* were entirely drawn from a single five-note (pentatonic) scale. Once he

began side-slipping, he continues doing so for the remainder of the fifth chorus.

8. At the beginning of the sixth chorus, the listener may notice that the repeating two-note phrase used there has a peculiar sound to it. It seems to be a three-note phrase, but two of the notes are the same, but with a different fingering, which changes the quality without changing the pitch. This device is called *vent-fingering*.

9. The whole sixth chorus is again based on the same pentatonic scale as before.

10. He returned to side-slipping in the middle of the seventh chorus.

11. The remainder of the solo was taken up with the pentatonic scale that cements together the motives of the album, along with an increased number of side-slips, some of which seemed to continue for a chorus or more, inordinately stretched in length. Notice that Trane used the full range of his instrument many times during the solo, from the lowest note on the horn to a note that is seven semi-tones higher than the natural range of the tenor saxophone.

COLTRANE DISCOGRAPHY

Africa/Brass, Impulse S-6

Africa/Brass, Vol. 2, Impulse 9273

Alternate Takes, Atlantic 1668

Art, Atlantic 313 (2 records)

Ascension, Impulse S-95

Avant-Garde, Atlantic S-1451

Bahia, Prestige S-7553

Ballads, Impulse S-32

Believer, Prestige S-7292

Best Of John Coltrane, Atlantic S-1541

Best/Greatest Years, Vols. 1, 2, 3, (2 records each), Impulse
   S-9200, 9223, 9278

Black Pearls, Prestige S-7316

Black Pearls, Prestige 24037 (2 records)

Blue Train, Blue Note 81577

Coltrane, Impulse S-21

Coltrane Jazz, Atlantic S-1364

Concert In Japan, Impulse 9246 (2 records)

Cosmic Music, Impulse S-9148

Crescent, Impulse S-66

Expression, Impulse S-9120

First Trane, Prestige 7609

Gentle Side, Impulse 9306 (2 records)

Giant Steps, Atlantic S-1311

Impressions, Impulse S-42

Infinity, Impulse 9225

Interstellar Space, Impulse 9277

John Coltrane, Prestige 24003 (2 records)

Kulu Se Mama, Impulse S-9106

Last Trane, Prestige S-7378

Legacy, Atlantic S-1553

Live at Birdland, Impulse S-50

Live at the Village Vanguard, Impulse S-10

Live at the Village Vanguard Again, Impulse 9124

Live in Seattle, Impulse S-9202 (2 records)

Love Supreme, Impulse S-77

Lush Life, Prestige S-7581

Master, Prestige S-7825

Meditations, Impulse 9110

More Lasting Than Bronze, Prestige 24014 (2 records)

My Favorite Things, Atlantic S-1361
Olé, Atlantic S-1373
Om, Impulse S-9140
Plays for Lovers, Prestige S-7426
Plays the Blues, Atlantic S-1382
Quartet Plays, Impulse S-85
Selflessness, Impulse S-9161
Soultrane, Prestige S-7531
Sound, Atlantic S-1419
Stardust, Prestige S-7268
Stardust Session, Prestige 24056 (2 records)
Sun Ship, Impulse 9211
Trane Tracks, Trip 5001 (2 records)
Traneing In, Prestige S-7651
Trane's Reign, Prestige 7746
Transition, Impulse S-9195
Two Tenors, Prestige S-7670

A
CHRONOLOGY
OF
JAZZ GREATS

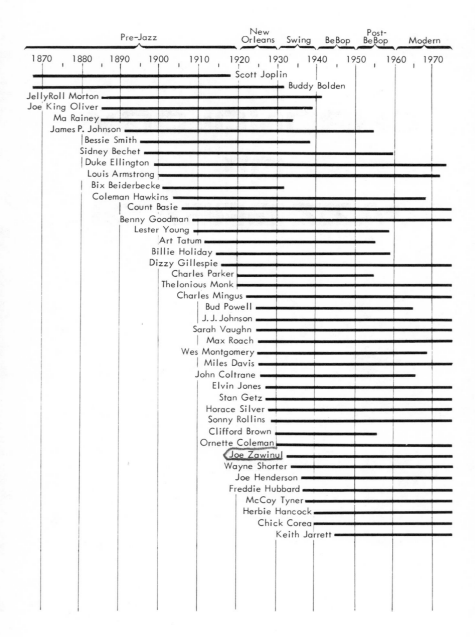

B

AN OVERVIEW OF JAZZ HISTORY BY PERIODS

PERIOD	YEARS	IMPORTANT PLAYERS/GROUPS	CHARACTERISTICS OF PERIOD
Pre-Jazz	1900–1920	Ma Rainey, Buddy Bolden, Scott Joplin, Huddy Ledbetter ("Leadbelly")	blues singers, ragtime, Creole influences, improvisatory marching bands.
New Orleans	1920–1930	Louis Armstrong, Jelly Roll Morton, Bessie Smith, Sidney Bechet, King Oliver, Bix Beiderbecke, James P. Johnson	blues singers, Dixieland sextets, early big bands (Fletcher Henderson and Duke Ellington)
Swing	1930–1940	Duke Ellington, Count Basie, Benny Goodman, Coleman Hawkins, Lester Young, Art Tatum, Billie Holliday	big bands, mass popularity, brilliant soloists, boogie woogie
Be-Bop	1940–1950	Charles Parker, Dizzy Gillespie, Thelonious Monk, Max Roach, Bud Powell, J.J. Johnson, Sarah Vaughan, Miles Davis	small groups, fast tempi, complex harmonies, sudden change to art music, decline in popularity and big bands
Post Be-Bop	1950–1960	Miles Davis, Sonny Rollins, Stan Getz, Horace Silver, John Coltrane, Elvin Jones, Clifford Brown, Ornette Coleman, MJQ, Charlie Mingus	cool jazz, longer solos, invention of modal tunes, beginnings of thematic improvisation
Modern	1960–	Miles Davis, John Coltrane, Herbie Hancock, Chick Corea, McCoy Tyner, Keith Jarrett, Mahavishnu, Billy Cobham, Wayne Shorter, Brecker Brothers, Stanley Clarke, Joco Pastorius, Joe Henderson, Woody Shaw, Freddie Hubbard, Wes Montgomery, Weather Report	contemporary and free form tunes, modal tunes, rock influences, electronic gadgetry, evolvement of jazz education

GLOSSARY

Many of the terms have more than one definition or various shades of meaning. The definitions given here will agree with the manner in which the terms have been used in this book.

ANGULARITY   use of wide intervals, abrupt leaps.

ART MUSIC   music which develops at its own artistic pace, with public consumption being a secondary consideration.

ATONAL   without a key. *? why? who wants it?*

BALANCE   relative audibility of individual performers within a group, achieved primarily by adjusting the volume levels of individuals until each part can be heard in proper proportion with all other players.

BALLAD   a slow to very slow tune, with respect to tempo.

BAR   measure.

BE-BOP TUNE   a tune fashioned after the jazz tunes of the forties, having a fast harmonic rhythm and frequent modulations to other keys.

BLUE NOTES   the lowered 3rd, 5th, and 7th degrees of a key.

BLUES   a vehicle that is indigenous to the jazz idiom, having its own distinctive 12-measure progression, utilizing blue notes, and sung or played with a tragi-comic flavor.

BOMB   a relatively unexpected drum accent, usually played on the bass drum.

BOOGIE WOOGIE   a unique piano style of the thirties, usually based on the blues, and having a left-band bass line that plays eight notes to the measure in an exaggerated swing style.

BOSSA NOVA   a tune having a type of Brazilian samba beat (felt in two slow beats to the measure) and a melody largely written or felt in steady, long, syncopated quarter notes.

BREAK   a point in an arrangement in which all instruments (including the rhythm section) suddenly cease to play for, say, two or four measures while the soloist continues to play alone, then the accompaniment resumes after the break.

BRIDGE   a contrasting section of a tune, usually a "B" section in structural terms, and generally occurring only once within one complete chorus. It is also called the *channel* or *release*.

CADENZA   a rather long *break*, but without a regular tempo-feeling, in which one player (the soloist) may play freely, while the other instruments remain silent or nearly so.

CHANGE-RUNNING   the practice of musically "spelling out" the notes of each chord in the progression in a rather continuous, nonlyrical fashion.

CHANGES   chords, chord progression.

CHANNEL   see *bridge*.

CHORD VOICINGS   the arbitrary spacing of the individual notes contained in an assigned chord.

CHORUS   one complete playing of a tune with all of its sections.

CHROMATIC   in semi-tones.

CLICHÉS   frequently-played ideas.

COLORISTIC DEVICES   sounds that generally avoid the mere playing of a chord or some other common function but add interest to the overall texture of the performance.

CONTEMPORARY TUNE a type of tune that generally has a less-predictable chord progression and uses unusual or less-common chord structures.

COUNTERPOINT simultaneously occurring melodies.

CUTTING SESSION a competitive jam session in which at least one player hopes to best at least one other player, usually by selecting difficult vehicles, keys, or tempi.

DENSITY relative quantity of notes.

DIGITAL PATTERNS a particularly chosen series of notes, often formulized in a numerical series, like 1–2–3–5 (for key universality), which can be easily transposed to any or all chords of a progression. Closely related to *change-running.*

DORIAN MODE a very popular scale for use in modal tunes, structured like a major scale that has been recirculated to the second degree of the scale. For example, a "D" dorian scale uses the notes of a "C" major scale (C–D–E–F–G–A–B–C), but begins on "D" (D–E–F–G–A–B–C–D).

DOUBLE-STOPS the simultaneous playing of two notes, especially on stringed instruments.

DOUBLE-TIME the interpretation of a tempo at twice its given speed, usually by doubling the note density.

DRONE an indefinitely sustained or repeated sound, functioning as a very light (usually), unchanging background.

DYNAMICS relative and graduating volume or intensity levels.

EMBELLISHMENT musical decoration of a note or phrase, accomplished by adding extra tones without obliterating that note or phrase or making it entirely unrecognizable.

EXTENSION adding of notes to the top of a chord, i.e., a 9th, 11th, or 13th.

EXTRAMUSICAL DEVICES sounds not normally associated with the instrument, without regard to exact pitches, melodies, chords, or the like, i.e., squeaks, vocal yelps, electronic feedback, etc.

FILL nonessential, but often very effective or functional, improvised accompaniment in spaces provided by the natural ebb and flow of the soloists' melodies. For example, as a horn might back (play behind) a singer, or a pianist might back a horn soloist, or a drummer might coach an ensemble.

FLURRY   a very rapid group of notes.

FREE-FORM   in its purest sense, unstructured or spontaneously structured group improvisation, though some organizational device (other than chord progression) is usually adopted to promote cohesion.

HALF-TIME   the interpretation of a tempo at one-half its given speed, usually by reducing the density to one-half its previous level. Sometimes referred to as "playing in 2."

HARMONIC RHYTHM   the rhythm established by the number and relative durations of the chords in a given progression.

IMPLIED BEAT   a consistent beat that is felt and understood, but not played in the consistent manner of time-keeping rhythmic figures.

IMPROVISATION   spontaneous or semi-spontaneous musical creation.

INTENSIFICATION   a raising of the energy level in music, usually accomplished by the coordination of factors like volume, range, density, tone quality, manner of phrasing, etc.

INTERLUDE   a transitionary section of an arrangement that is not a consistent part of the vehicle's chorus structure, often used to lead into an important solo entrance or to help effect a change of mood, relieving monotony.

INTERVALS   measured distance between different notes.

INTONATION   the relative precision of pitch.

JAM SESSION   a musical rap session, often between players who do not play together very often, if ever, focusing on improvisation and without arrangements, though mutually known tunes will be selected along with some effort to create a spontaneous arrangement.

KEYNOTE   the tonic note ("1") of a given key—in other words, the lettered name of the key (i.e., the keynote in the key of "C" is C).

LEAPS   wide intervals; see *angularity*.

LYRIC   the words or text to a song.

LYRICISM   the quality of intense melodiousness.

MEASURE   the space between vertical bar-lines in notated music. The bar-lines group beats together in specific, consistent numbers. For example, in common 4/4 time, each measure has four beats.

MELODIC DEVELOPMENT   the retention, usually in terms of successive variations, of a particular motive or fragment of a melody.

MELODY CHORUS   the chorus, generally heard at the beginning and end of a jazz selection, in which the given melody is played.

MODAL TUNE   a tune that has very few chord changes, each with extremely long durations (slow harmonic rhythm), and is treated as a scale, usually dorian (see dorian), rather than chords.

MOTIVE, MOTIF   a very brief, but significant, melodic fragment of perhaps 2–6 notes.

OCTAVES   notes that are eight scale tones apart, bearing the same letter name.

OSTINATO   a repetitive accompaniment figure, usually retained throughout the performance of the selection.

OVERLAPPING   the practice of beginning a phrase shortly before an important downbeat of a new section or chorus, continuing the phrase across the dividing line and into the next segment, obscuring somewhat the fact that a new section has been entered.

PATTERN-PLAYING   the adopting of formulized realizations of chords and scales, such as digital patterns (see *digital patterns*).

PENTATONIC SCALE   a five-note scale, digitally represented as 1–2–3–5–6 of a major scale.

PITCH   a particular vibrational frequency or, in the vernacular, a "note."

PLAYING INSIDE   improvisation in which all notes selected are contained within the given chord or scale.

PLAYING OUTSIDE   improvisation in which few, if any, of the selected notes are contained in the given chord or scale.

POLYCHORDS   the simultaneous occurrence of two or more different chords.

POLYMETRIC   the simultaneous occurrence of two or more time signatures (meters).

PROGRESSION   the entire sequence of the chords contained in one chorus of the tune. Sometimes called *changes*.

QUOTES   melodic phrases in an improvisation that have been borrowed from a different tune altogether.

RAGTIME, RAG   a unique piano style of the late 1800s and early 1900s, which was generally written rather than improvised, using much rhythmic syncopation and a long, multisectioned formal structure. It wielded a strong influence on early jazz.

RANGE   the distance between the lowest and highest notes of an instrument or voice.

REGISTER   a term used to approximate various levels of range in a comparative fashion, such as low, middle, or high registers.

RELEASE   see *bridge*.

RESOLVING TONES   two successive notes, one from each of two successive chords of a progression, which sound unusually logical, and smoothly connected in sequence.

RHYTHM SECTION   a group of instruments within a jazz ensemble, usually piano (and/or guitar), bass, and drums, which form the more stable, consistently present part of the band, supplying chords, bass line, time-keeping figures, and suggestions and responses to the soloist.

SCAT VOCAL   an improvised jazz solo by a singer, usually without words, and often in imitation of an instrumental jazz solo.

SEMI-TONE   the smallest stable interval between any two notes. In a continuous chain, they would produce the chromatic scale (i.e., C, C#, D, D#, E, F, F#, G, G#, A, A#, B, C).

SET-UP   a rhythmic figure played by a drummer to make it easier for an ensemble to play phrases accurately, with the set-up occurring just before the ensemble enters with the phrase.

SIDEMAN   any member of a group, except the leader.

SIDE-SLIP   a deliberate but unassigned shift to a sharply contrasting chord, scale, or key, usually employing melodic symmetry.

STANDARD TUNE   a tune, particularly those of the thirties and forties, which was once a very popular song and then becomes a perennially played tune.

STOP-TIME   a long series of *breaks*.

TAG   a short extension of a tune's length, usually lasting 2–4 measures.

THEMATIC IMPROVISATION   see *melodic development*.

TIMBRE   tone quality.

TIME SIGNATURE   a numerical symbol of the number of beats in a measure and the value of the note that will receive one beat of duration.

UNISON   simultaneous singing or playing of exactly the same notes by two or more people.

VAMP   a repetitive accompaniment figure, usually as an introduction.

VARIATIONS   melodies or melodic fragments (motives) that closely resemble a previously played phrase but are slightly different in some way.

VEHICLE   a tune selected for improvisation.

VIBRATO   a regulated wavering of pitch on a sustained note, warming its sound. It closely resembles the *tremolo,* which is a regulated wavering of amplitude (volume).

WALKING LINE   a bass line that moves like a scale, four notes per bar.

WHOLE-TONE SCALE   a six-note scale made up entirely of wholetones (two semi-tones) or whole-steps between each of its adjacent scale degrees.

see over →

Shadings   "size"

THINGS TO DO

FOR "Book"   Lyricism

DATE Riffs

	ITEM	FINISHED
1	"Head" arrangement	☐
2		☐
3	IRT Subway to	☐
4	Harlem	☐
5		☐
6	Voicings	☐
7	tonal textures	☐
8		☐
9	shuffle style (Savitt)	☐
10	720 (in the Books)	☐

Special Arrangement

DEA
DISC
RE
AN

Record Haven
233 West 42nd St.
New York NY 10036

The Record Exchange
842 Seventh Ave.
New York NY 10019

Harry Berliner Music Shop
154 Fourth Ave.
New York NY 10024

The King's Voice
P.O. Box 45
Massapequa Park NY 11762

S.H. March
Discount Record Shop
Swynned Valley PA 19436

8313 Shawnee St.
Philadelphia PA 11918

Parkside Radio and Record Shop
696 Flatbush Avenue
Brooklyn NY 11225

The Record Album
254 West 81st St.
New York NY 10024

Disc-O-Rama
107 North George St.
York PA 17401

146

Records Unlimited
P.O. Box 510
Carnegie PA 15106

Colony Records
1671 Broadway
New York NY 10010

Chamber's Record Shop
97 Chambers Street
New York NY 10007

Sam Goody
235 W. 49th St.
New York NY 10019

King Karol's
111 W. 42nd St.
New York NY 10036

Record Hunter
140 W. 57th St.
New York NY 10019

Liberty Music Shops
50th St. & Madison Ave.
New York NY

Music Masters Uptown
25 W. 43rd St.
New York NY 10036

H. Mielke
242 E. 86th St.
New York NY 10028

Berlitz School of Language
52 Broadway
New York NY 10004

Wally's Stereo Tape City
11th Ave. near 47th St.
New York NY

Darton Records
160 W. 56th St.
New York NY 10019

Four Continent
5th Ave. at 22nd St.
New York NY

French Book House
62nd & Lexington Ave.
New York NY

Metro Music Co.
54 Second Ave.
New York NY 10003

Spanish Music Center
319 W. 48th St.
New York NY 10036

The Record Undertaker
P.O. Box 437
New York NY 10032

Discontinued
216 N. Rose
Burbank CA 91505

RCA Cutouts
Box 566
Massena NY 13665

Apex Records, Inc.
947 U.S. Highway #1
Rahway NJ 07065

Dave Bryant
Tacony Distributors
4421 Ridgwood
St. Louis MO 63116

Harry Warriner
Knickerbocker Music Co.
453 McLean Ave.
Yonkers, NY 10705

Candy Stripe Records, Inc.
17 Alabama Ave.
Island Park NY 11558
516–432–0047

The Golden Disc
228 Bleecker St.
New York NY 10014
212–255–7899

House of Oldies
267 Bleecker St.
New York NY 10014
212–243–0500

Syble's Golden Oldie Records
5417 E. Lancaster
Ft. Worth TX 76112

J.T.'s Record Shop
662 E. 38th St.
Indpls., IN 46205
317–926–7235